Gray Highway

GRAY·HIGHWAY

an american ufo journey

matthew holm & jonathan follett

toadspittle hill productions, llc • new york

Toadspittle Hill Productions, LLC
Radio City Station
P.O. Box 1846
New York, NY 10101-1846

Library of Congress Catalog Card Number: 98-86502

ISBN 0-9666044-0-7

Printed in the USA by Morris Publishing, 3212 E. Highway
30, Kearney, NE 68847; (800) 650-7888.

Acknowledgments

Thanks to the International UFO Museum and Research Center in Roswell, N.Mex., for permission to publish the interior photography on pages 95, 97, and 98 and the "alien autopsy" photograph on the front cover.

We would like to thank Hunter Boyle for the P.E.E.R. photography on pages 231, 234, and 236.

Special thanks to Jennifer Hagendorf for her research and marketing work and to Brian Dawson for his help with copy editing and fact checking.

And, we would like to thank our families, our friends, and our girlfriends for their patience and support.

Introduction

Much has happened in the two years since we first embarked upon this project. The UFO phenomenon has experienced a groundswell of popularity. Roswell, N.Mex., has celebrated the 50-year anniversary of the most publicized alleged UFO landing in history, with enough hoopla to warrant a cover story in the June 23, 1997, issue of *Time* magazine. *The X-Files* has grown from a cult television murmur into the number one movie in America. Will Smith has cemented his acting career with two hit alien movies. And for $1.50, you can purchase glow-in-the-dark alien lollipops at the corner convenience store. The national attitude toward UFOs has changed so much, in fact, that one conspiracy theory purports the United States government is behind the alien fever infecting American popular culture: Numerous leaks to a rabid media and a Big Brother-esque influence on the Hollywood movie machine are government PR tools used to prepare the public for an inevitable extraterrestrial arrival.

Whatever the case may truly be, in the midst of the capitalist siren call, it's easy to forget that the UFO phenomenon is a distinctly human one, as well. For every sighting there is a witness, and for every abduction a victim or willing participant. And then there are the UFOlogists, the psychologists, psychiatrists, and hypnotists, the entrepreneurs, the reporters, the cranks, and the crazies. Mix well, salt to taste, and scatter across America. Mark where they land, see where they live, and draw a route to connect them all together. Then drive. This is the Gray Highway.

Jonathan Follett, Matthew Holm
New York, N.Y., June 25, 1998

Table of Contents

960305

Prologue
The White Mountains, New Hampshire
March 5, 1996
M.H.

The rustic, cabin-cozy barroom of Frannie's Place in Thornton, N.H., is a welcome change from the treacherous mountain roads we've been driving, snowblind, for the past five hours. I've taken my Geo Prizm into what is arguably one of the worst snowstorms of the season so that I might retrace the path of Betty and Barney Hill on the night of their alleged abduction by UFO occupants some 35 years ago. Why? UFOs and outer space have always interested me, and I figured that I should finally get some firsthand knowledge of the phenomenon. With me is one of my roommates from Penn State, Joe Koon, who's just along for the ride, glad to make an otherwise housebound day into an adventure. (We came to Boston for spring break to visit my friend, Jon Follett; Jon, who

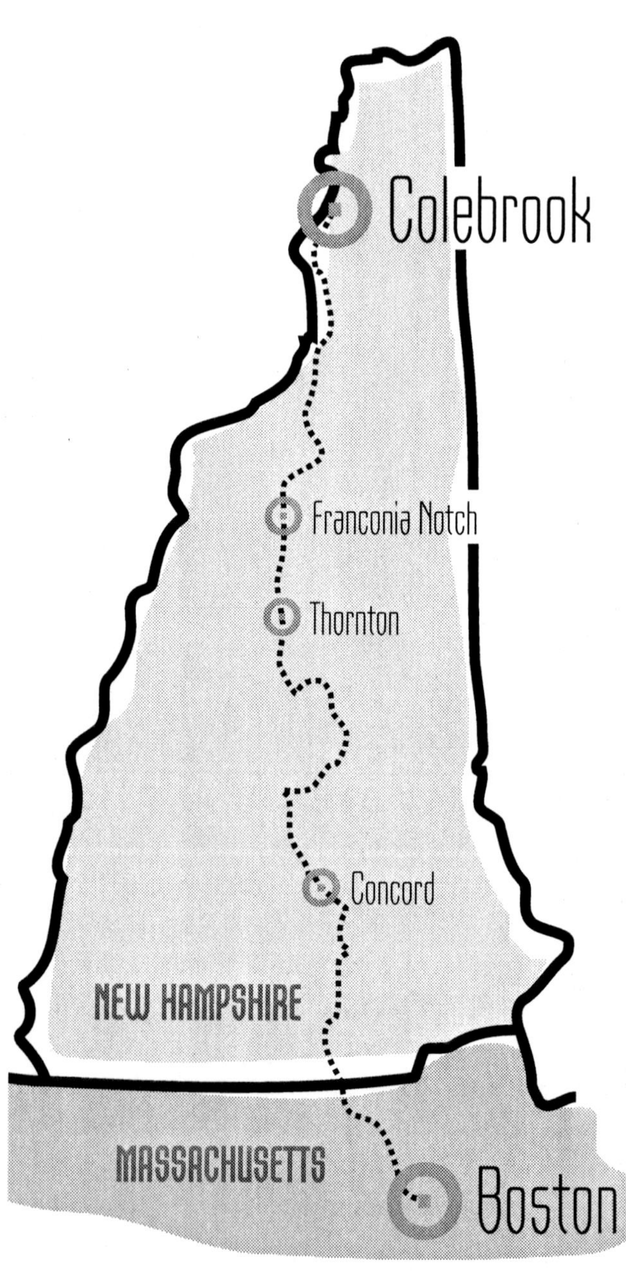

Colebrook
Franconia Notch
Thornton
Concord
NEW HAMPSHIRE
MASSACHUSETTS
Boston

will accompany me on the month-long UFO-hunting odyssey we've planned for this summer; Jon, who is busy today. Joe was kind enough to fill in for this single trip that I somehow decided, upon awakening to a growing snowstorm, would be a good way to spend the day.)

Although the restaurant is virtually empty, its main dining rooms left dark and vacant by the postseasonal lull, Frannie's is still a peaceful retreat from the nerve-racking roads and is a foothold of American civilization. The short, cheerful woman in her late thirties (presumably Frannie) who greeted us and waits on us, the nameless cook we know only as a noise in the kitchen, the lone, drunken customer (probably also in his thirties, though he looks much older), and the babbling TV mounted near the ceiling reassure us and remind that, though we've seen nothing of it for many hours, the real world still exists outside this snowbound, depopulated, wooded wilderness.

The man at the bar laughs over slurred inconsequentials with Frannie, spilling a total of three beers during the course of our stay. He comes over to our table briefly, and we learn that he works as a baker for one of the big resort restaurants nearby. On a drunken sidetrack about the area's seasonal homeowners, he also confides that "Rich people don't love their homes like I do." Joe and I nod and hmm at him and then order a pizza and some caffeine from Frannie. The crazy rantings of a drunk are a warm, welcome touch of humanity.

I soak in the plain comfort, the sheer ordinariness of it all, and worry a little that our trip might not yield any excitement. After all, we can't expect the UFOs to show up just because we do. But now I hear the words coming from the TV and realize that Fate is playing funny little games with us. I catch the teaser of a tabloid TV show as it goes into a commercial break. Coming up next: people who believe that they're extraterrestrials.

Think of the chances—if we had left Boston half an hour earlier or later, or if Frannie had preferred *Wheel of Fortune* instead, we might have missed it. I can't even comprehend what the logistics would have been for planning how to leave Boston, drive on unknown roads through a sudden blizzard, fight random traffic as schools close and businesses empty unexpectedly early, and arrive at Frannie's exactly during the 7:30 to 8 P.M. block—much less figure out how to make the whole thing coincide with a network's broadcast schedule for a two-minute segment that could easily have aired any other day of the year. The break ends and the segment shows a bunch of pretty ordinary-looking suburbanites talking about how they're actually ETs that were born into human bodies. One man says that he's 25,000 years old. "Now, it's people like that who give the UFO community a bad name," Frannie chimes in. "Come on. Twenty-five thousand years old. Now me, I'm just 16,000 years old."

Joe and I share a laugh with her over that, but the drunk, who up until this point has been laughing at most anything, becomes as sober as he is able. "I've seen aliens," he tells us, quite seriously. "I saw them walking down the hill over there toward the lake. No one else saw them—they said they just saw a light. They said it was from the factory or something, but, uh-uh. They were real and I saw them." That pretty much kills the conversation, and he returns quietly to his beer as Frannie brings out our pizza. We finish eating and leave, slightly uneasy.

By 8:30 we're on the road once again; on slippery, snow-covered roads, and, what's worse, on U.S. Route 3. To follow the Hills' journey as closely as possible, we chose Route 3 rather than I-93, which meant choosing an unplowed, two-lane road with 35 MPH maximum safe speeds over its well-tended, wide-laned, speedy parallel.

Even setting aside the need to encounter a spacecraft and suffer an abduction, our trip can never duplicate the Hills' exactly. To begin with, the time of year is wrong—we're six months out of sync. The Hills never had to contend with these driving conditions. The roads they drove that September night disappeared because they had their memories erased, not because it was snowy. What's more, Joe and I started the day in Boston, rather than in Canada. The Hills had begun their short vacation four days before the September 19, 1961, encounter and had spent some time in Niagara Falls before returning east, passing through Montréal and heading south down Route 3 on that last night, through Colebrook, N.H., the White Mountains, and Concord, N.H., on their way home to Portsmouth.

There are also similarities: Both trips began on something of a whim, with Joe and me deciding only this morning to make the drive and Barney suddenly arranging a few days off from work and packing Betty and their dog, Delsey, into the car for a short vacation in Niagara Falls. And while we aren't driving at the same time of year, we are, like the Hills, between seasons. Two tourist seasons, summer and winter, fill the White Mountains with life. In summer, boats ply the lakes and hikers take to the mountain trails while families get bogged down in the tourist traps. In winter, skiing makes the forbidding, deadly peaks into cozy hideaways: well groomed, well lit, and well traveled. Surprisingly little has changed in 35 years.

The Hills had just missed the summer crush and were far too early to witness the winter wonderland that the mountains would become. We, on the other hand, have just missed the end of the formal skiing season—as has the snowstorm we're driving through. Plus, it's midweek, and what few skiers might still be coming would likely wait until the weekend. As we dip through the mountain passes, row after row, lot after lot of speedboats stand at the roadside, entombed in their winter tarpaulins. They stand poised, lined up like call girls for the vacationers who will come and use them in a month or more, bouncing them across the waters and then returning them at day's end for the next man in line.

We soon approach the most significant stretch of highway, the touristy area near Woodstock, N.H., known as Franconia Notch. Above us, visible only as black silhouettes against the overcast charcoal sky, the granite cliffs have been weathered into recognizable shapes—Cannon Mountain, shaped like a jutting gun barrel, and the Old Man of the Mountains, an anthropomorphic rock that serves as New Hampshire's state symbol. Not that we can make out any such details in the dark. We stop at the only motel on the whole strip that seems to be open and look at some brochures and postcards in its lobby to see what we're missing (not much). Back outside, I strain to extract a form from the dark, vague shadows towering to the west, but with no success. I imagine the Hills had similar luck on their night drive (when their attention wasn't fixed on the light in the sky, that is), though they had at least visited the area before.

We experience their journey in reverse. First for us is Franconia Notch, where (reconstructed through subsequent drives as well as hypnotic regression therapy by Boston psychiatrist Dr. Benjamin Simon) Barney drove down a side road, the car stopped, and aliens helped the suddenly drowsy Hills from their car and up a ramp into the spaceship.

The event supplied a number of milestones: the first reported alien abduction, the first use of hypnosis to recover repressed memories of a UFO encounter, and even the first application (by Dr. Simon) of the term "abduction" to describe the contact experience. It also may have been one of the earliest Earth missions by the alleged UFOnauts: While they clearly had their trademark techniques down—erasing memories, stopping vehicles, talking with their eyes, collecting sperm and ova—the visitors still seemed to know very little about human beings. The crew was astonished by Barney's dentures, and immediately checked to see if Betty's teeth were also removable. And, in a conversation with Betty, the leader was stumped by a wide range of human concepts, including aging, time, food, and color.

A bit further up the road for us, though we can't say

exactly where, the Hills made their first stop after sighting the UFO in the sky. They had been watching the strange light as they drove and finally pulled off to get a better look at it and let out Delsey—who was suddenly squirming and whining and going out of her little doggy mind—for a walk. The craft drew very close, and Barney, walking a ways off from the car, peered at it through his binoculars. He saw the craft's crew at a large window, and locked eyes with the leader. The contact sent him running and screaming back to the car, and he quickly drove away with Betty and Delsey, the specter of those compelling eyes still before him.

We see moose danger signs as we drive. The markers warn of the hundreds of accidents and deaths caused every year by moose. And we hear not alien voices in our heads, but French on the radio—Quebecois DJs playing techno and industrial dance music on AM radio. We wind further through the hills and past desolate valleys scraped clean by glaciers, in wilderness, the northern frontier of America, yet only a scant few miles from the beginning of Canada. Finally, we roll into and out of Colebrook, the far endpoint of our journey, and turn around.

We find no diner to match the one the Hills describe (but how many restaurants from 35 years ago have remained unchanged, or even open?), so we stop at the only place that seems to be open: the Colebrook House Hotel 'n Lounge. A sign reading "Welcome—Bienvenue" beckons us in. This is the sync point for the two trips, where Joe and I turn around and start moving in the same direction as the Hills. It's 10:50 P.M. as we enter the restaurant—

we're a mere 45 minutes behind their schedule.

The barroom seems like the set of a David Lynch film. The only light comes from neon beer signs and overhead fluorescents that have all been replaced with black lights. Half a dozen people sit quietly at scattered tables. A drunken fat man and a small woman, grossly mismatched in size, feel the lure of the adjacent parquet dance floor and are soon waddling to the music. Joe orders coffee and I order a Coke, in the hopes that we might not fall into a daze on the highway like the Hills did, and we get out as quickly as possible. The paranormal oddities don't let up as we leave, though, for I notice flyers announcing the upcoming "Psychic Weekend at the Colebrook House," promising tarot, astrology, numerology, and free lectures this coming weekend.

We've come a long way from the days of the Hills—now, backwater hotels can host psychic weekends as casually as a bingo night, and hypnotic regression is performed on everyone and his grandmother (which, I guess, makes sense since alien abductions seem to run in families). Back in the day, things were a bit more grave. Reporting UFO sightings was bad enough, but claiming actual contact with extraterrestrials was really asking for trouble. Such misfortune and public embarrassment eventually befell the Hills when, years after, a reporter outed them in a series of articles about their experiences.

When they arrived home from the White Mountains early on the morning of September 20, 1961, the Hills remembered only the sighting and were aware that they could not recall a two-hour period, marked at either end by a series of beeping sounds. They made the proper reports to the police, Air Force, and to investigators from Project Blue Book (the government-supported program that documented UFO sightings in the 1950s and 1960s), and went about their business as usual, save for Betty's abduction nightmares and Barney's worsening ulcers and anxiety.

Barney's health problems eventually led to psychiatric sessions, and after some time, his doctor suggested that, as a side issue, the Hills should look into hypnotic regression therapy to explore the missing time on their journey, since the event was still very much on Barney and Betty's minds. They were referred to Dr. Benjamin Simon, a psychiatrist who had used hypnosis and drugs like sodium pentothal to effectively treat amnesia and anxiety resulting from battle fatigue (post-traumatic stress disorder in our day) during and after World War II.

Reading the account of Dr. Simon's treatment in John Fuller's book, *The Interrupted Journey,* the contrast between regression therapy then and today is astonishing. Simon could not have cared less whether or not Barney and Betty had been aboard a spaceship. He was surprised, to be sure, when they recounted such events under hypnosis, but that wasn't his problem. He wasn't even after the truth about what happened that night: All he cared about was treating the Hills' anxiety. Dr. Simon spent a great deal of time preparing himself and the Hills for the sessions, even getting them used to being in trance states, before he tried to extract any information under hypnosis. And even afterwards, he struggled with allowing them to hear the recordings of the sessions (for he had instructed them not to remember, upon waking, anything they had said under hypnosis until he told them to), for fear of the damage it might cause them.

(Dr. Simon was very skeptical about UFOs. His conclusion, which he admitted was uncertain and problematic, was that the shock of seeing a strange object in the sky caused the Hills' amnesia and that Betty's nightmares, when recounted to Barney, infected his psyche and they both then recalled them as "real" events. This was the only hypothesis—apart from the possibility that the abduction actually occurred, something Dr. Simon couldn't accept—that he felt would explain the unerring similarity of their separate accounts.)

Today, many regression hypnotists are not psychiatrists, and do not take quite as much care with their patients. Granted, they are offering a lower-cost solution than psychiatric care, and often try to act quickly since many abductees must take time off from work and travel from far away to get treatment. Also, very few traditional psychiatrists accept the reality of or are equipped to deal with abduction scenarios, and patients may feel their physicians are less than sympathetic toward them. But in the end, the focus of much modern, non-psychiatric hypnotic regression is to uncover traumatic abduction experiences that were buried (buried perhaps with good reason, since such memories can cause a great deal of pain if recalled), rather than to heal the patient. Many professionals are cautious about using hypnosis, and remind that it is by no means a proven way of discerning truth. Indeed, patients can lie or confabulate (that is, make up and then describe false memories) when under hypnosis. And most of all, they note the danger of being hypnotized by someone who is not professionally trained, for the operator may not be able to appropriately handle the strong emotions the session may evoke in the patient.

As we drive back, still on the safe side of fatigue, we scan the dark, featureless skies for stray lights. I think of the many ways the Hills described and accounted for the UFO. First, it was merely a bright star, then possibly a satellite. Next a plane, perhaps a piper cub (Barney was an airplane enthusiast, which was why he carried binoculars in the car: to watch planes; the absence of engine noise throughout the sighting troubled him deeply). Finally they saw it as a cigar-shaped object, or more accurately, once they were close enough to make the distinction, a lens-shaped craft seen edge-on. In their conscious screen memories (memories constructed by the brain to make sense of the nonsensical, or to disguise and repress a potentially hurtful event) prior to undergoing hypnosis, the Hills recalled seeing the moon sitting on the ground. After regression, they decided that "the moon" was actually the brightly lit craft, just before it took off into the night.

Consider this, then, as we now approach Franconia Notch once again and see, for one of the few times all night, headlights in our rearview mirrors. The lights gain on us slowly, sometimes hidden momentarily by a rise or curve in the road, but always following. Joe and I wait for them to close in and pass, but they suddenly fall back and veer off to the right of the road.

"Holy shit!" Joe exclaims, whipping his head around.

The road, you must understand, is completely fenced in for miles by guardrail. On this stretch, *there is no place to turn off.* No side roads. No shoulder. Only guardrail flanked by a dropoff of unknown depths and the forest beyond. We slow the car and look back, waiting for the headlights to catch up, to reappear and swing around into a U-turn, or to be swallowed by flames and billowing smoke from a crash—anything—but the mysterious lights have vanished without trace. Joe's gotten his money's worth on this little jaunt. We drive on, pass beyond the perilous guardrails to more open, level country, and see no more of the ghost car.

The night wears on, and although the ghost car still haunts my memory, I begin to despair of seeing a good, old-fashioned UFO. It seems that, maybe, those 45 minutes made all the difference. Perhaps, in 35 years, the aliens have figured out the concept of time and now demand punctuality.

With our eyes fixed on the charcoal sky, we nearly miss the strange visitor right in front of us. I slam on the brakes and stop a dozen feet from a female moose that probably outmasses my car. She stands in the opposite lane, grazing at weeds near the edge of the new snow. With grass hanging from her mouth, she swings her head towards us and stares, seeming rather bored.

Just as with lights in the sky, sightings of alien beings can generate screen memories. Most common among these are images of animals, often the wide, relentlessly staring eyes of owls or deer. I've never heard of a moose in such a context before, but for me, it's close enough to

Frannie's Place

a deer to be worrisome. The one reassuring thing is that the moose's gaze does not seem especially intense. Her half-lidded eyes barely register recognition of the hunk of metal next to her, and she waits to finish up her snack before ambling unhurriedly off the road and into the nearby woods.

We pull out slowly, hardly believing what has happened, and press ahead to Boston. I feel content that we have at least one encounter under our belts—a foretaste, maybe, of the longer UFO pilgrimage my friend Jon and I will make this summer. But as it did for the Hills, the remainder of the drive becomes hazy in my mind as fatigue weighs on me. Betty and Barney didn't fully recover their senses until they reached Concord, and so it is with us, the fog only lifting when we stop there for gas. Early morning brings us to Jon's apartment in Boston, and I tell him of our encounters and the unnerving events of the long, snowy night. We can only imagine what awaits us under strange, hot, summer skies.

Skywatch and the Earl of Gulf Breeze

Gulf Breeze, Florida
May 26, 1996
M.H.

On the narrow beach of Shoreline Park South, it's just before dusk. This is the time when extraordinary things usually start to happen in Gulf Breeze. Ed Walters, the Gulf Breeze builder who took dozens of photographs of UFOs in 1987 and 1988, had most of his sightings at dusk or dawn. Eight years later, on the Sunday of Memorial Day weekend, Jon and I have arrived in the early evening, before sunset, to see some unexplainable sights of our own.

Before us stand two specimens: one man, in his fifties, with wild gray-white hair and mustache, glasses, and a lavender T-shirt stretched tightly over his belly, and another man, forties, with a bicycle, puffy red face, and wide, unblinking eyes. Both seem to be experiencing other realities.

The staring man mumbles how he rode his bike across

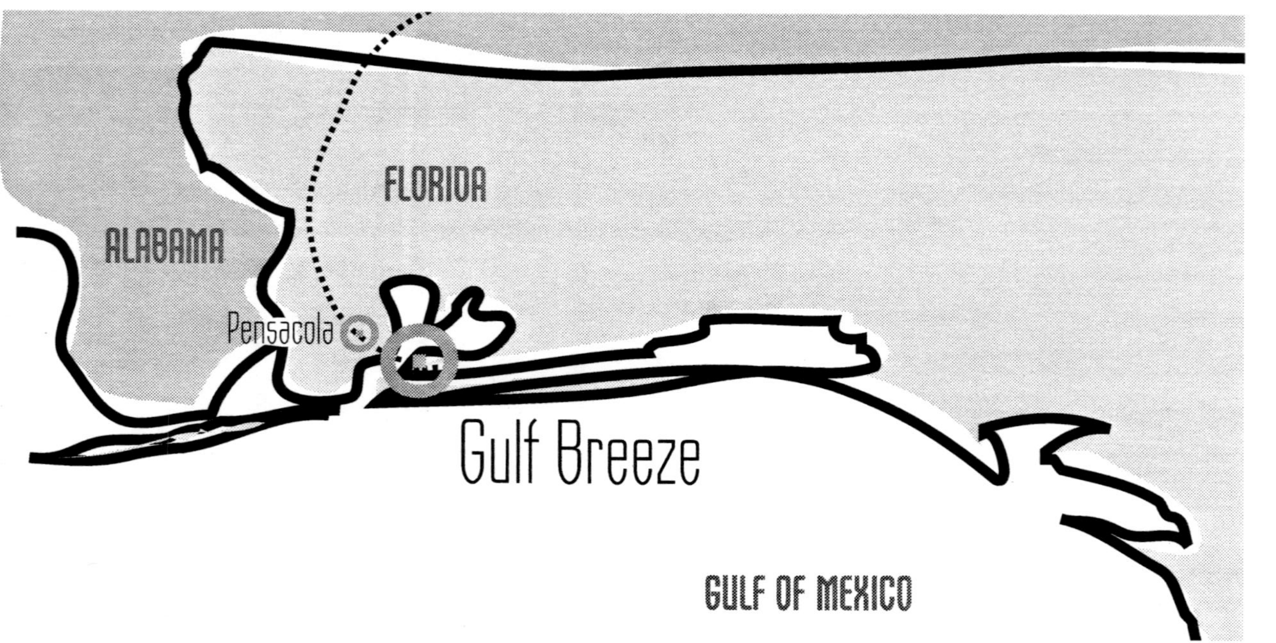

FLORIDA
ALABAMA
Pensacola
Gulf Breeze
GULF OF MEXICO

the three-mile long Pensacola Bay Bridge early in the day, but is now afraid to go back across with night approaching, afraid that the drivers will have a hard time seeing him. He sniffs frequently and stares and stares at nothing in particular. Rather than brave the traffic, he decides to sleep on the beach, curling up on the bench of a concrete picnic table in the late afternoon light, a towel draped over him as a blanket. A short time later, evidently finding the accommodations not to his liking, he wanders off.

Earl, the other man, doesn't seem to be a local, but rather from Ohio. I think. Trying to follow him becomes maddening, as he cannot stay on one story and can't make any of them clear. Of Ed Walters, he says, "He's the guy with the ideas—in that book." I chicken out and shoot some video of the surroundings, leaving Jon to do the preliminary interviewing. Jon returns a few minutes later, shaking his head. "Dude, that guy—," he sighs, exasperated. "Twinkle twinkle!"

These bathrooms are neon green, folks.

We had hoped to find Bruce and Ann Morrison of the Gulf Breeze Skywatch here, rather than the glue-sniffer and twinklehead, but it's still early. I reached Ann by phone yesterday around noon, while we were still working our way through Alabama, and she told me that she and her husband are at the Park most every night, and that we could meet them there.

The trusting nature of people sometimes shocks me. Some guy claiming to be a writer calls her up on her home phone number, which he got God-knows-where (the Internet, actually, where the Morrisons were listed as contacts for Gulf Breeze Skywatch), and she gives him her probable whereabouts. Who are we, anyway, that she should tell us?

Lucky for her, we're two fairly harmless recent college grads (Jon from Boston University and I from Penn State) who went to high school together in the suburbs of Philadelphia. We had originally planned, last summer, to go cross-country with a convoy of our college friends as a postgraduation road trip, but by the fall we noticed that no one else was saving cash, no one else was planning, and no one else had considered a way to get their own car (we can only fit our gear and ourselves into my Geo Prizm). It was then that we agreed to plan the trip as though everyone else would bail. And so they have.

A "working vacation" would be one way of describing this trip, but it would be a poor one. Thus far, it's been mostly work (or at least grueling monotony on the road)—not vacation. But that's our fault, and our deliberate choice. Since no one else is coming along, and we can certainly get our act together and get things done, we reasoned, why not *really* get something done? So rather than just drive to cool places around the United States, we narrowed our focus, in an elegantly entrepreneurial way, to something we could write about and sell. Some of the locations we had originally intended to visit—including Roswell, N.Mex., and Area 51, Nev.—are UFO-related sites. With just a little more planning (OK—a LOT more planning) we restricted our trip to sites within the 48 contiguous states that are home to some of the milestones or big stories of UFO history: Roswell, N.Mex., the possible crash site of a flying saucer nearly 50 years ago; Rachel, Nev., the closest town to the barely secret military base at Groom Lake known as Area 51; Mt. Rainier, Wash., where Kenneth Arnold spotted the first UFOs of the modern era and the term "flying saucer" was born; and many others, including Gulf Breeze, for some 20 in all.

Some will turn out to be newsworthy, others may be mere tourist traps or even impossible to find. But finding them is not entirely up to us: We shared the problem with the poor cartographer down at AAA, who needed two days to assemble the hundreds of pages of our Trip Tik, which is as thick as a best-selling paperback. Maps, guidebooks, road atlases, and books of background information make up a significant portion of our cargo.

The car is full. We packed enough clothes so that we will only have to do laundry twice. On our feet are Doc Martens, the toughest boots known to us. (Today I wore crappy sneakers to the beach; a welcome respite as I've been breaking in a new pair of Docs for the past few days. Jon brought two old pairs, and fully expects to wear out one set during our travels.) To preserve our sanity, a few cubic feet of the car is devoted to storing tapes and CDs, and a chunk of our budget is earmarked for batteries for the portable CD player. To document our experiences, we packed notebooks and a Macintosh PowerBook for writing, several audio tape recorders for interviews, two 35mm cameras for stills, and a camcorder compliments of my sister, Jenni.

Three days ago, when we packed up the car and left our parents' homes in Audubon, Pa., we had hoped to be packing up and leaving in a baby-blue, 1965 Chevy Nova, also borrowed from my sister. She had purchased it for $50 from a New York City Police auction (its previous owners—from California—failed to pick it up after it was towed), so if the car died on the road, it wouldn't be too great a loss. It would have been a really romantic car to take on a road trip, an American-made steel monster with a beaten-down interior, an AM/FM radio stuck permanently on one frequency, and no air conditioning. Perhaps luckily, Jenni became too attached to the car to condemn it to our evil wills, so we opted for my Geo Prizm. Not a bad alternative, since it's only seven months old and gets good gas mileage, has all the amenities (air conditioning), and is painted a rich grape color to boot. We fear the poor thing may not be quite so young and innocent after 12,000 hard and dusty miles.

So far, the miles have been a bit soggier and more winding than I expect those to come shall be. Rain dogged us on and off for the last three days as we made our way down Skyline Drive in Shenandoah National Park and the Blue Ridge Parkway further south in the Smoky Mountains. The first morning was sunny and clear, but late in the day, rain slowed the already-slow drive through the mountains. Our campsite in western Virginia had miraculously dried out by the time we pitched the tent, but the night hosted its share of discomforts.

As anyone undertaking a trip such as this will soon learn, where you sleep is directly related to how much cash you have. We have about three or four thousand bucks between us—not nearly enough to stay in even the cheapest motels every night on the road, or eat every meal in a restaurant. And while it may work for students in Europe, in America there just simply aren't enough youth hostels to get you across the country and back. We plan to stay at only one, in New Orleans, tomorrow night. Most of our nights will be spent sleeping in a tent and cooking on a Coleman stove, the consequence of which is that the tent, tarps, poles, pegs, hammer, shovel, ax, rope, sleeping bags, stove, propane, pots, pans, plates, utensils, cooler, food, and water that we're bringing takes up the majority of our trunk and backseat.

Thus we learned the first lesson of the trip: You have to unpack and re-pack everything you bring, every single day. Worst of all, we learned it in a mosquito-infested wilderness where we couldn't stay outside or leave any food even briefly uncovered after nightfall. Dinner was cooked hastily and then eaten in the tent. This cocooning protection backfired on us in the middle of the night, however, when Jon—who has only slept in a tent once before—deliriously woke, his face in the nylon, and suffered a panic attack, thinking that he was trapped in a plastic bag or an alien pod of some sort.

The next day brought the worst rain I've ever driven through, conveniently while we were descending from the highest point of the Blue Ridge Parkway. It was an exhausting, arm-tensed half hour down followed by another half hour of completely blind driving as night fell and the storm picked up. We stayed in the Sunset Motel in Murphy, N.C., for a blessedly low $35.

Pensacola has more than depleted that blessing, though, since the Memorial Day crush of shore vacationers has all but filled the motels here (an unfortunate coincidence of timing—we left the first day possible after moving Jon from his apartment in Boston and gathering all of our gear). We paid $143 for two nights (pretty awful considering the previous two nights combined cost us a third of that) at an ironically named Econo Lodge, and set about scoping out the area.

Gulf Breeze is a narrow strip of land anchored by bridges to Pensacola on the mainland and Santa Rosa Island on the Gulf side. The UFO sightings here have been called the best-documented, largely thanks to Ed Walters, who diligently took Polaroids of the craft and even agreed to use a special sealed camera designed by the Mutual UFO Network (MUFON), a private UFO investigative group with chapters worldwide. His photographs—more than 40—as well as his 1-minute, 38-second videotape of a UFO have stood up to every proof, and photo analysts remain convinced that they were not faked.

The majority of Walters's experiences took place around his house, located a short distance from Gulf Breeze High School, which we passed on the drive in. But it's a private residence, of course, and Ed Walters has tried to remove himself and his family from the public spotlight and return his life to normal. We won't go there. But we can visit Shoreline Park, where Walters, the Morrisons, and others have seen and videotaped UFOs on hundreds of occasions.

This morning we scouted the Park, which has two distinct sections: the community center, a large building with gymnasiums and outdoor recreation facilities, and Shoreline Park South, a narrow beach with picnic areas just down a short sandy road from the community center on Shoreline Drive. The daycare center there proved particularly revealing. From the roof of a covered pavilion just outside, a piñata twists slowly in the ocean breezes.

Gulf Breeze High—home of Ed Walters' UFO sightings

La piñata del astronauta

The odd thing is that the piñata is no horse, donkey, pig, or other common creature, but a silver-suited spaceman gripping a ray gun. Are the daycare workers trying to acclimate children to the sight of extraterrestrials, or rather putting a stick in their hands and teaching them the proper way of dealing with alien invaders?

Shoreline Park South is a pleasant (if not a little boring) spot to take the family on a sunny afternoon. The main section, flanked by parking lots, stretches for less than 50 yards along the water and maybe 30 yards back. The actual sand on the beach is a few scant yards wide, and a wooden pier stretches out into the shallow water. Except for the Florida heat and subtropical plants, Shoreline Park South could easily be confused with any lakeside beach further up the continent. It's not, after all, on the ocean. Without UFOs to draw a night crowd, the place would be pretty quiet.

Well, relatively quiet. When we were there earlier today, we shared the beach with families picnicking at the tables, kids casting nets into the gentle waves to catch unknown seafood—and jet skis roaring up and down the water. The early afternoon proved sunny and pleasant: fine for taking pictures, but far too loud, thanks to the jet skis, to get any decent sound with our videotaping. Jon and I returned to our hotel, napped and ate, and hoped that the evening would bring less water traffic and more air traffic.

• • • • •

Shoreline Park was quiet ... too quiet.

As we watch and film the lights on the water now—lights from anchored boats, the homes across the sound, the bridge, and occasional planes—a powerful breeze that has accompanied the fall of darkness fills in nicely for the jet skis, rumbling past the microphone over which we've hastily taped a couple of (clean) socks to form a windscreen. It seems to be the one accessory my sister forgot.

Jenni works for a small production company in Manhattan and was able to get us a Canon Hi-8 camcorder plus three batteries, a charger, and some 20 hours of tape. Shoot everything and ask questions later. (She has a friend working on some new show for Comedy Central called *The Daily Show* that starts later this summer, and the woman sounded interested in what we're doing. Maybe something will come out of it.) The camcorder records at broadcast quality, but the sound may not turn out as well. After all, cinematography, sound, and directing fall mostly on my shoulders (Jon has the unfortunate job of having to be witty and photogenic for the next five weeks). We have no boom man, no professional foam windscreen, and almost no microphone: The short shotgun-style mic is badly dented and barely attached to the camcorder, having been slammed in a car door sometime during its life at my sister's production company. We let the video work consume us for a while, taping shots of the beach, the water, Jon walking through the moonlit surf, and so on, biding our time until any of the indigenous Skywatchers appear.

On the western side of the Park we spy four heavyset middle-aged women in polyester pants and floral-print shirts sitting in lawn chairs. I introduce myself and ask if any of them have seen UFOs here in the Park. Sadly, no. They're cheerful and friendly, though, and one goes on to describe how, when she was visiting her sister in Idaho, she saw a UFO "shaped like a sperm" cruising over the Grand Tetons. These ladies aren't part of the Skywatch—they're just out for a pleasant evening. Ed Walters, they tell me, doesn't come out to the Park much since all the initial attention, but the Morrisons do. One of them motions past me and I realize that the Skywatchers have arrived.

On the opposite end of the beach, Bruce and Ann sit in folding lawn chairs, staring out at Santa Rosa Sound. Both must be in their fifties or early sixties. Ann is small and thin with short golden-white hair, glasses, and a sleeveless shirt and shorts, both pink. Bruce, with curly, graying hair and glasses, looks like Kurt Vonnegut. At their feet, a nervous, hyperactive, skinny puppy weaves through the sand. A few middle-aged men stand nearby, poring over a Florida road map on the hood of a car with a flashlight. They call Bruce over to discuss certain Gulf Breeze sightings, and he points out the location of landmarks: a Kmart; a lonely convenience store. Ann stands to walk her dog, taking off her shoes and stepping into the surf.

I feel uneasy intruding on this little group, much as I would not want to interrupt a family gathering. Solemn and separate, the Skywatchers appear to enjoy their privacy. But it *is* a public beach and they *are* listed as contacts, so Jon and I sidle closer. The Morrisons don't even blink at a couple of UFO researchers, and Bruce calmly tells how he and Ann spent nearly every night from 1990

a night at shoreline park

a night

at shoreline

park

960526

to 1992 on this beach. He is nonplussed by his 285 UFO sightings, lacking even the enthusiasm and wonder of a veteran bird-watcher. "They've been quiet lately," he notes. Ann seems more concerned with her dog than with UFOs or UFO researchers. Tonight marks the first Skywatch for young "Sassy," an anxious pup with short golden hair. "I feel relaxed with a dog on the beach," Ann says. "Right. Natural." The duo is pretty cool about such an incredible phenomenon, but after six years even lights in the sky must get old, as must the endless questions from journalists and transients.

Since not every night's research will yield results (Although I am told that if you visit the Park for ten nights in a row, you're almost guaranteed a sighting), the Skywatch inevitably has to become a sort of mellow beach party. If you don't enjoy being on the beach at night when UFOs are absent, the Skywatch is going to get old real fast. When one of the men breaks out a portable radio, I almost wish I had brought a six-pack to share. Everyone gathers around the picnic table and listens to talk radio.

Area 51 and reverse-engineered flying saucers are the subject of the paranormal call-in show. The loopy show is made significant for us when Glenn Campbell, director of the Area 51 Research Center in Rachel, Nev., calls in. Glenn is a skeptic and government gadfly who moved from Boston to the trailer community of Rachel in order to check out Area 51. Jon and I plan to hit Nevada in two or three weeks to chat with Glenn and take a peek at the base. On the radio, Glenn states briefly that most people see what they want to see at Area 51, mistaking fighter jets and military flares for flying saucers. He finds more believable the stories of reverse-engineered alien craft at S-4—a military base located at Papoose Lake, well to the south of Area 51 and much better hidden from public view—than the tales of UFOs over Rachel.

The Skywatchers listen with interest, the men sometimes smiling or chuckling at various comments. In another place and time, these people would probably be hanging out and laughing at a local pub, the VFW, or an Elks Lodge or some other club. Jon and I are strangers to their establishment, treated politely but not really a part of the community. I feel a little uncomfortable, but then Earl the Twinklehead pipes up and puts things into perspective. We may be new to the pub, but at least we don't act like drunken fools.

First Earl brings up a particular video he had recently seen, and the Skywatchers, having seen it, declare it to be a bunch of nonsense. They don't think much of his sources.

Then Earl says, "They live for thousands of years, you know."

Tom, one of the Skywatchers, looks at him quizzically. "Who?" he asks.

"The aliens."

"Where did you hear that?" Tom presses.

Stammering follows as Earl, seemingly unaccustomed to even the simplest skeptical inquiries, sifts through his addled brain for the appropriate source. All he can come up with is, "It was in that book, with the ideas." Earl, it seems, has a few too many ideas.

An uncomfortable moment follows as the Skywatchers consider how to rid themselves of this crank. It's all too much for Bruce and Ann, I think. As they didn't bring a video camera with them, I sense they had just planned to spend a quiet holiday evening on the beach—one that we (and Twinkletoes) have cut short. The Morrisons are soon gone; they leave so fast that Ann forgets her sneakers. I spot the shoes in the sand and pass them along to the remaining Skywatchers, then decide to rid these folks of their Earl-burden.

Jon and I pull Earl aside for an exclusive interview, much to the amusement of the Skywatchers. Sure, he's no UFO authority or reliable witness, but since he is a part of the phenomenon (hell, he's almost a phenomenon himself), he's important to us. Leave no stone unturned, no wacko unexamined. We lead him under the orange lights near the parking lot and roll camera.

Jon forgoes opening questions, knowing that Earl will do us proud if left to his own devices. "Earl's going to tell us about his sighting experience," Jon says to the camera. "Take it away, Earl."

Earl stares at the ground for a moment, lost in thought. In the artificial light, his pinkish shirt now looks a dirty gray. Once he finds his way out of his maze of ideas, in his slow, quiet, twangy voice he recounts his sighting on the road from Crestview, Ala., to a place just south of Nashville. "It's a place called—it's like an Indian name," he says. "What the heck was it? Gosh. Anyways, it's the name of the lower Florida area Indians." From the backseat of a car, riding with his cousin and a friend, Earl spotted lights in the sky that he assumed were from an airplane. "So I made a joke, 'Hey—there's a UFO!'" Earl chuckles. "Yeah!"

As Earl and company drove closer, he discerned the object's shape as "two triangles, put together." The craft—flat—was covered on the bottom with gray blocks. "There was a light in the center, more or less, protruding out, but you couldn't see nothing but the umbra of the light itself," he recalls. "But above it there was like red lights, similar to what they had on TV a while back where they saw it over in England."

"Uh-huh," nods Jon. "And how long did you see this for?"

"This was somewhere around two and a half years ago," says Earl, misunderstanding. Jon doesn't stop to correct him. "I was just, uh, not thinking about UFOs or anything," Earl continues, "but I saw this one and as we came up to it, that's when it hit me: It was hovering. Wasn't flying toward us or nothing. The speed, uh, as big as it was, it seemed like it had the speed there."

"And it just disappeared?" asks Jon, trying to get something more coherent from him. A "yes" or "no" would be

"Take it away, Earl!"

Earl describes the motion of the UFO he saw.

fine, but Earl refuses to be led.

"It was an area—a creek—it was similar to a bridge but it was like a solid bridge," he says. "Water was underneath, going through a collar—uh, rocks or something like that—so you couldn't really tell like a regular bridge, a trestle bridge or something like that. All it had was guardrails." Clearly the bridge was not like a normal bridge, but what that has to do with the UFO disappearing, I can't figure.

"Anyway," he continues, realizing he should make some sort of point related to Jon's question about the craft's activity, "this thing was on the left of that, and as I was looking at it, the weird thing was, it was staying up there like I said, and then all of a sudden as I was looking at it, it started banking off—like a piece of paper would come out of your hands. But it was gliding. It was real weird, coming off to the side." For a brief moment I think Earl can pull it off, can say something meaningful, for he's describing an often-reported UFO behavior known as a "dead-leaf maneuver," where the craft drifts sideways like a falling leaf, either while it seems to be trying to maintain a stationary position or when descending the last few feet to the ground. But then Earl throws in, "It wasn't forward or backward or anything like a regular UFO or something."

A regular UFO?

Jon, equally bewildered, asks, "So it just went sideways?"

"It just went sideways," says Earl. "And it was too big to be a helicopter."

"And you're convinced it was a UFO, then."

"Yeah, I think that's what it was," Earl says, his voice trailing off a bit, "'cause it looked so much like the one I saw on TV."

"And now you're down here with Skywatch, I guess," says Jon, "checking out the—,"

"Yeah." Earl smiles sheepishly.

"—checking to see if you can get another sighting."

"I had a friend of mine, a while back who saw one. This was back in the '50s, when I saw this," he says, then pauses. "Well, I didn't see it," he corrects, confusing himself with his friend. The sighting took place in Newtown, Ohio, where both Earl and his friend lived at the time. "Him and this other friend were down there wrestling, in front of a appeals office," he says (wrestling in front of the appeals office—I picture some sort of primitive frontier justice), "and this thing was out on a road, like, away from the main road. His house was off to the side of all this. So. A light was shining above the house, shining a light *into* the house. This, you know, was a light—as far as what we could see, a light—a UFO because of what he said.

"And the weird thing was, by the time he finally got out of the wrestling ideas and went up to his house to show it to his dad," says Earl, "it started going away."

Wrestling ideas?

"The thing he told me about it was, as far as he was seeing and saying it was at about, say 400 yards," he says. "And at that speed and everything—he went up to his house, and it was hovering above his house—it didn't have no sound. This was back in the '60s when I heard this."

"Right," says Jon, wrestling with Earl's ideas himself. "Wow."

"Early nineteen sixty … two or three," Earl says, clarifying possibly the only point of his testimony that didn't require it.

"Well, thanks a whole lot," Jon says with a hearty handshake. "We really appreciate it." Earl smiles, not realizing how important he has been to our investigation—truly, in the tangled tapestry of the UFO phenomenon, as central a figure as any of the skeptical and experienced Skywatchers.

Walking back to the car, bathed in amber streetlights, Jon and I pass a bunch of teenagers who are hanging around their cars, smoking cigarettes and drinking beer: High school kids who have tomorrow off. They eye us lugging our cameras and bags, and a girl calls out, "What are you guys doing?"

Jon and I have asked ourselves that question over and over for the past week while packing, driving, and filming. What the hell are we doing? Why do we want to look for UFOs? We aren't hard-core UFO researchers (or UFOlogists, if you wish) like the many that currently populate and push the boundaries of this most pseudo of all sciences, nor have we suffered any sort of abduction experience or even once spied a strange light in the sky.

But although we're skeptical, we're keeping our eyes peeled. For all the trouble we're going through for this trip, we'd like to see some cool stuff by the end.

While we go to look for UFOs, our eyes are really trained Earthwards. Regardless of whether or not we believe in or have seen (or believe we have seen) alien visitors, there are plenty of people out there who do believe. We want to find those people, for the odds are pretty good that they will be at least as interesting and unexpected as anything dreamt up by science fiction novelists, apocalypse-fearing religious dogmatists, or conspiracy buffs. We're curious to see how the people living at the UFO sites view their homes, their lives, UFOs, and the fools like us that drive into town to take a gander. We want to find the kings of UFOdom, the knaves, and the Earls. If the UFO phenomenon is legitimate or a hoax, if lights in the sky are really spacecraft or the planet Venus, if abductions are a product of alien geneticists or troubled psyches, it doesn't matter: Whether real or fake, the phenomenon still affects millions of people.

I sling the camera bag into the backseat and—not wanting to go into all of our reasons, motives, and methods—simply tell the girl, "Filming." Jon starts the car and we pull out, more than enough material on tape and ideas in our heads for one night. Although we spied no lights in the sky and may never know firsthand the truth about Gulf Breeze's night fliers, we've gained a much clearer notion of what really goes on down here on the darkened beaches.

Maybe the truth is out there. But we're after something better than the truth.

03

Burning Cars & Rotting Fish

Pascagoula, Mississippi
May 27, 1996
J.F.

Matt and I are headed for Pascagoula, Miss. When you say "Pascagoula" out loud and emphasize the last two syllables—Pas-ca-GOU-LA—the town's name sounds like the perfect setting for a trashy B-grade horror flick, equal parts blood and schlock. The same feel applies to the trip so far. We're caught up in an adventure that is incredibly serious and frightening in its implications, but equally comical and ridiculous in its execution.

We're journeying to a spot where two alien abductions allegedly took place in October, 1973. The abductees, Charles Hickson and Calvin Parker, were fishing on a shipyard dock when a UFO appeared and neckless aliens with long arms and pincers for hands descended upon them. This was one of the earliest abductions ever documented.

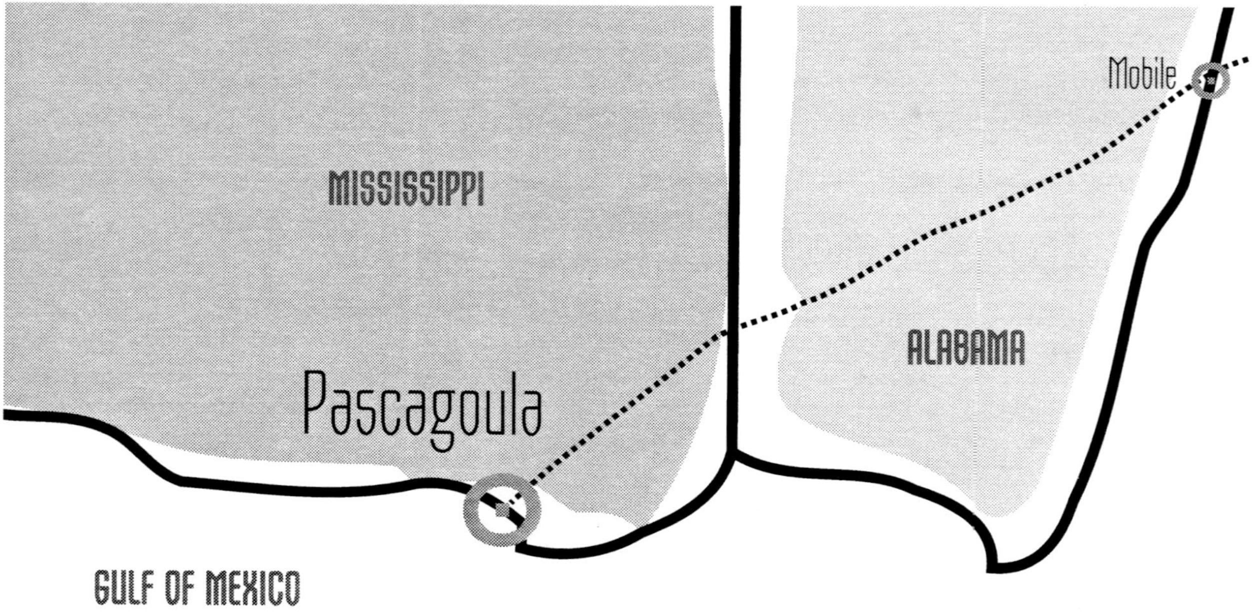

MISSISSIPPI
Pascagoula
ALABAMA
Mobile
GULF OF MEXICO

We are 20 miles from Pascagoula when we notice, by the side of the highway, an enormous smoldering black scar, obviously the remains of some great fire. The long grass has been burned away for 50 feet or more all the way to the tree line. A fire truck is parked, waiting faithfully for its owners who are, no doubt, off making sure that the conflagration has truly expired.

Images of downed spacecraft dance through our heads. Could this be the next Roswell? In moments the military will be here to cordon off the area and keep back the press. We've got to get some footage. We stop the car, pull the video camera from the back, and march bravely toward the still smoking ground. I play tour guide Geraldo for the camera, giving the blow-by-blow for our nonexistent audience. The sound of the cars whizzing by us on the highway melts together into an ocean-like roar and, for a moment, I'm high on the hope of making first contact.

Car fire or cover-up?

Car fire.

A figure emerges from the woods to our right, and we're disappointed to see that, rather than a pincer-equipped alien, it is merely a worn-out fireman wearing coveralls and a bright T-shirt. We hustle to intercept him before he reaches his vehicle.

"What's going on?" I yell above the noise of the traffic.

The fireman takes one look at us, shakes his head, and keeps walking. "It's a car fire," he says and waves us away.

Is this a cover-up? we wonder. Matt and I are up for a good conspiracy theory but there's no sign of any camo-clad gentlemen about. We glance through the trees and see two more fire engines next to what seems to be the remains of a car. So much for the spaceship. We clamber back into the Geo and continue our trek to Pascagoula.

Around lunchtime, we finally reach the shipyard. We're not sure if it's the same place from which Hickson and Parker were abducted, but since we're 20 years removed from the incident, a close approximation will have to do.

The sky—a chilling murky gray—is filled with clouds. A few seagulls lazily glide through the air, occasionally calling to each other in a helpless, sighing tone. As Matt and I step onto the docks, our nostrils are immediately assaulted by the stench of rotting fish. This will be a short investigation, we decide. To our right, industrial cranes stretch their steel arms to the sky. To our left, a motorboat plods through the water. We both agree that the aliens couldn't have picked a more boring place to stage their sinister deed.

The place feels abandoned, like the soul has been washed out of it, and the UFO trail seems cold. But somehow I know we're on the right track.

Soulless Pascagoula

The Price of Truth

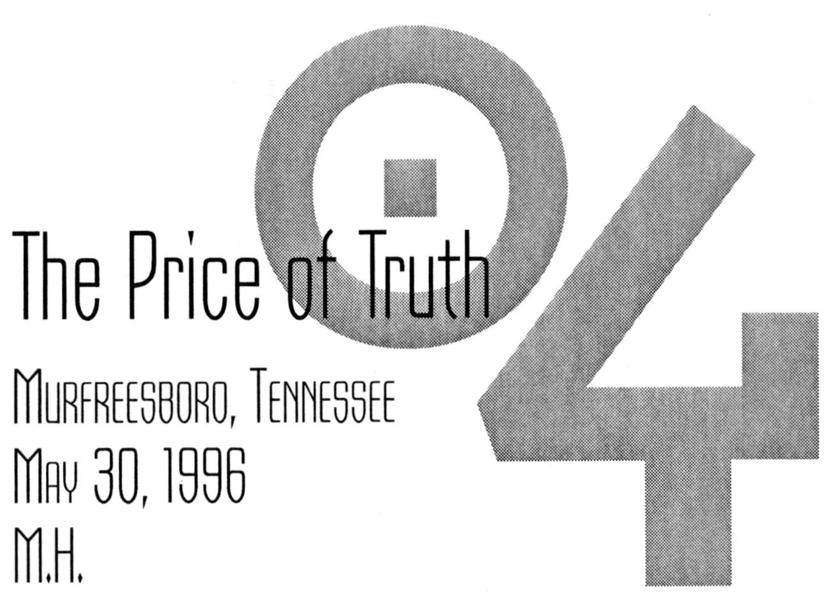

Murfreesboro, Tennessee
May 30, 1996
M.H.

As I ask the waiter for two checks, Leah Haley and her husband, Marc Davenport, freeze in horror and then dive back into their menus to see what they can afford. When they decide to split a meal, Jon and I know that things are not off to a good start. We know that this interview will not be about Leah's abductee books or her mail-order company, Greenleaf Publications. It will be about money.

It's not that Jon and I hadn't discussed buying dinner. When Leah told me over the phone that she would try to bring her husband along, it set us into tortured debate: Do we pay, or don't we? In the end, we decided to pay for Leah if she was alone, and let them take care of themselves if Marc came, too. After all, what if they decided to bring all their nieces and nephews? Would we pay for

gray · highway

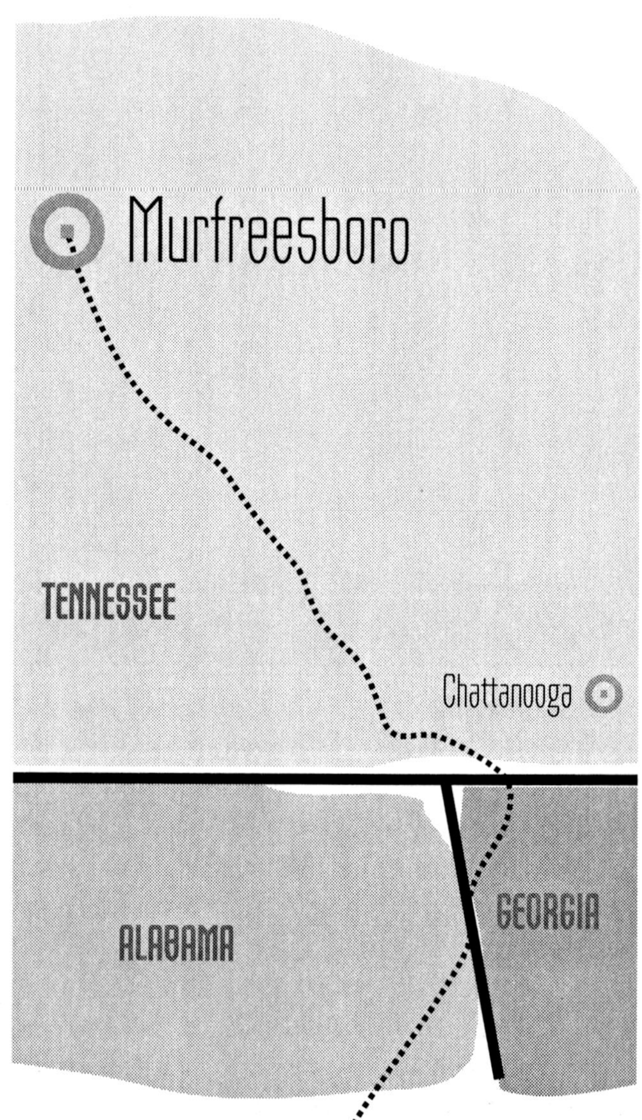
Murfreesboro
TENNESSEE
Chattanooga
ALABAMA
GEORGIA

them, too? We have no reason to speak with Marc—all we want is Leah.

Leah wrote *Ceto's New Friends,* a children's storybook about alien abduction, and Marc—well, Marc came with her. We don't know what he's done. He's her husband, but that doesn't mean we should pay for his dinner. We're writers. We're starving and suffering for our art. We're going to be out at least $3,000 for this moronic trip. We're doing the right thing.

We're about to get lectured.

Here we are, two professional, college-educated adults who are not new to interviewing or writing, and Leah's husband—some guy we don't know, didn't invite, and don't have the slightest idea as to why we should pay for his dinner—starts to lecture us on proper interview etiquette. Marc gently chides us for our obvious inexperience and explains that, when people usually conduct interviews, the researcher compensates the subjects for any time they have to take off from work—or at least pays for their meal. All well and good, except that in the dozen or so interviews I'd previously conducted, that had never been the case. And if we're getting into the value of someone's time, then I think that the biologists, engineers, and cancer researchers for whom I'd never bought a meal rated slightly higher than two mail-order booksellers.

Marc concludes his speech and Leah suggests that we rewind our tape recorders and start over. I'm flabbergasted, but what can I do? Too stunned to think of faking it—fast-forwarding the tape instead of rewinding—I follow Leah's instructions and obliterate the juicy quotes. She is a woman who claims her mission is to disseminate the truth about her experiences, yet she orders me to cover up the unpleasant episode. A bloody start: With the proof destroyed and only three dinners on the way, we begin the documented portion of our interview.

Leah is a small woman with short, dark hair and glasses, wearing a short-sleeved top and dark blue jeans. She appears to be in her late forties or early fifties. Being an author and a bookseller is at least her third career: She first got a master's degree in education and taught English (grammar and literature), then went for an MBA and became a Certified Public Accountant. It was while she was working as a CPA and teaching college-level accounting that she began to uncover her history of alien abduction. In the shakeup of her life that followed, she lost her job, got divorced, and eventually married Marc Davenport, who we learn is an author, UFO researcher, and former engineer. He's tall and lean with dark, moppy hair and a beard, wears jeans and a T-shirt, and looks to be at least ten years her junior.

The two of them live here in Murfreesboro, Tenn., about an hour south of Nashville, where they run Greenleaf Publications, a catalog bookselling operation and publishing house that specializes in paranormal titles. Greenleaf will sell you any book that's in print in the United States; it also is the imprint for Leah's books as well as one of Marc's. Leah has written two books about alien abduction.

"We weren't taught about aliens," Leah says in her

twangy Alabama voice. "I wasn't. I wasn't taught about aliens in my *church*. I wasn't taught about aliens in my *school.* I got lied to. I felt cheated when I found out that there were aliens. My first experience was when I was three years old. The first one I can remember." She wrote *Ceto's New Friends* so that other kids—and adults—will not be as traumatized and confused when they are abducted. "The way I see it," she says, "if you're educated about the existence of something, you're not going to be as afraid as if you have some kind of experience when you know absolutely nothing about it."

Ceto's New Friends serves as a primer for young abductees. Illustrated by Lisa Dusenberry (a member of MUFON who helped Leah deal with her own abduction) in a heavy-handed style, the story's poorly rendered colored pencil drawings follow the exploits of Ceto, a Gray (one of the race of big-headed, dark-eyed aliens that have gained increasing press in recent years), who travels to Earth and meets two young children, Annie and Seth. Ceto talks to Annie and Seth with his eyes, asking if he can play with them. The three diminutive characters play ball and shoot marbles (one wonders if the anatomy of Ceto's hand makes playing marbles easier or more difficult)—all pretty harmless until Ceto asks the kids to go for a ride in his spaceship.

They beam up, but Ceto's toys aren't really as cool as you might expect—think about being allowed to play in a car. The kids push buttons and watch computer readouts, then start to get drowsy. Ceto finally deposits them back on their green lawn and they exchange gifts: The kids give him a great little latticinio glass marble, and he gives them a mysterious purple rock (scientists must be itching to get their hands on THAT piece of physical evidence). The chilling last line reads, "The spaceship flew away, but Ceto will come back soon to visit his new friends on Earth."

"I have been praised—highly praised—and I have been criticized—highly criticized," says Leah. "I have not met anyone yet who has had a middle-of-the-road opinion. People either love it or they hate it. The people who criticize me say things like, 'Why do you tell kids to go off with strangers?'" A good point. The book is problematic: Reading it, I can immediately see her good intentions, but I simultaneously recognize the scary, unintended double meanings. Specifically, most adults assume that kids aren't going to be able to discriminate between hopping in a stranger's car and hopping in a flying saucer, though if actually placed in each situation, no person on the planet—no matter his age—would probably confuse the two experiences. "The book is not about strangers, it's about aliens," Leah says. "And anybody who reads it can see that quite clearly."

Not that you should want to throw in with every ET you meet. "Sure there are bad aliens," Leah says. "There are also good aliens. And it wouldn't be fair to write a book scaring people to death of all aliens, because some of them aren't bad. It's like, you wouldn't teach kids that all men are horrible just because a few have raped somebody. Or murdered somebody." That will be the *real* historic moment—not the first time aliens and humans make contact, but the first time an alien sues for libel.

"Ceto is the name of a real alien," she says—the one that's been in charge of her during the course of her life; Leah's case worker, so to speak. "I don't know if you spell it that way or not." *Ceto's New Friends* is loosely based on Leah's first abduction experience. "There is some fiction," she notes. "It is a fictional book. I wrote it in a fictional manner so that people who have no interest in the phenomenon would buy it and read it anyway so that it would sort of familiarize kids with aliens." She pauses as the waiter sets down the three meals and an extra plate. "So some of it's fiction," she continues. "Some of it really did happen to me. Like, there's a light that shines down from a spaceship, takes the kids up. That's real. The aliens talk through their eyes. That's real," she says. "But I did it in a manner that was nonthreatening."

Also fictionalized were the names: "Annie" for her and "Seth" for her brother, who really did share in the experience with Leah. She also gives him the pseudonym "Seth" in her first book, *Lost Was the Key,* a nonfiction account of Leah's awakening to the reality of her abductions. *Lost* shows her abduction experience to be thoroughly typical: Her close encounters began early in childhood; the abductions run in her family; in 1990, a skeptical, seemingly innocent investigation into the subject of alien abduction uncovered horrifying evidence that she was one herself; she experienced sleep disorders, physical illness, missing time, electrical disturbances, and found mysterious scars; finally, she recovered submerged memories both spontaneously and through hypnotic regression sessions with therapist John Carpenter (not the horror movie director), who was referred to her by famed abduction researcher, author, and artist, Budd Hopkins. These investigations cost her thousands of dollars in fees, phone calls, and travel expenses; she makes a point of warning others who wish to explore their own experiences that the truth does not come cheap.

As a result of all this, her life fell apart. Leah is convinced, both by odd daytime encounters and by some of her recovered memories, that she has been followed, bugged, drugged, threatened, and poisoned by the U.S. military/government (or, as she refers to her tormentors in the book's final pages, "OMAGS"—short for "obnoxious military and government scoundrels"), possibly because she was found aboard an alien craft that was forced down by the military near Gulf Breeze, Fla. Under hypnosis, she remembered snatches of a night when she stood on a beach in pajamas, her head hurting. An alien craft lay nearby, a gaping hole in its side, and soldiers rounded up her and a number of injured aliens, then took her away for interrogation.

Leah is most often visited by aliens she describes as "chalky-colored"—the short, large-eyed Grays like Ceto—though she's encountered a number of different types. "I think, six or seven," she says. "I'm starting to lose count." She counts them off on her fingers. "Chalky-colored. Teacher. Angel-like being. Rubber baby doll. Reptilians. Pleiadeans. And Sinéad O'Connor. One reminded me of Sinéad O'Connor," she laughs. "Seven!" The teacher, a taller and wiser version of the chalky-colored aliens, instructs Leah in various things that he generally won't allow her to consciously remember. Reptilians and Pleiadeans are both common figures in UFO lore, the Pleiadeans often described as tall, Nordic-looking humanoids who are basically good and the reptilians as, well, reptilian-looking creatures that are basically evil.

I ask what she thinks the aliens' agendas are—if they're all here for the same reason or not. "If my hypothesis is correct then they could be coming from a million different places," Marc chimes in. "They could have a million different agendas." Marc has also written two books: *Dear Mr. President,* a book of letters to send to people at all levels of authority in order to save the environment, and *Visitors from Time: The Secret of the UFOs.* Of *Dear Mr. President,* Marc says, "You can actually tear the letters out and send them, or, the copyright's written in such a way that you can lift a whole paragraph out and put it in your own letter and you're not violating any copyright restrictions." *Visitors from Time* explores his hypothesis that UFOs are actually vehicles designed to manipulate time as well as space. Changing the flow of time relative to such a craft could result in UFOs' peculiar behavior: traveling at thousands of miles an hour through the atmosphere, stopping and turning on a dime, emitting bright light and intense radiation, and vanishing into thin air. Likewise, it could explain why UFOs and their occupants exhibit such a variety of behaviors and appearances. The pilots could come from any planet at any point throughout history for any number of reasons (conquest, scientific study, petty theft, a vacation), and they could even be human—hence their interest in us, since we might be their ancestors. "So when we say, 'Why don't *they* do this or why don't *they* do that, what *they* are we talking about?" says Marc. "We have to talk about one faction. There's a whole bunch of them, from different places, and they all have a different reason for being here."

Many people believe that the aliens are not even material beings, but rather spiritual ones. Jon begins to tell Leah about a program we recently saw on a Christian cable network, where someone was equating aliens with agents of the devil. "You saw my mother!" Leah interrupts, laughing. Growing up in Alabama, Leah was raised in the Southern Baptist church. I ask what her beliefs are today. "I believe in God," she says. "I believe in Jesus. I believe in Jesus as the Son of God. However...." She trails off for a moment, thinking.

"Really, there isn't a conflict—in my opinion," Marc says, turning to Leah, "I think in yours, too—between Christianity or any of the other major religions and the fact that we're being visited. For instance, nowhere in the Bible does it say anything about this being the only planet where people are. But many places in the Bible, it does hint toward there being people on other worlds. 'In my father's house there are many mansions,' and so on."

"When I was growing up in the church," Leah says, "we were taught not to think, really! I mean, you just accept it, and you don't question. We weren't encouraged to think."

"It would be extremely arrogant of us—," says Marc, "even if we are devout Christians, if we believe that God created the Universe—it would be extremely arrogant to believe that He created billions and billions, as Carl Sagan likes to say, of planets and only put intelligent life on one planet. That's so arrogant. I can't believe we would think that."

But Leah's mother is the sort of person who does think that way. She's adjusted very poorly to Leah's experiences. "I've had a lot of problems with my mother," Leah tells us, "who says 'Stay away from those UFO people! They're bad, they're bad. They're demonic. And maybe some of them are."

Lost Was the Key ends too soon, really, for as Leah tells us about her life since she began investigating her abduction history, I realize that the last act takes place after the book's conclusion in January 1992. "I never told anyone about it," she says, "until I made the mistake of telling my boss and he fired me." Leah lost her job, then she lost her husband: She had begun speaking publicly about her experiences, much to her husband's chagrin. Not only did he disapprove of her speaking out, but he was also a little bit scared of her: Once, Leah tells us, he got caught in the aliens' beam of light and was almost sucked out of bed with Leah. "He was holding on to the bed post," she says, his feet straight up in the air. He later told her that he "kicked her out of his life" because he was afraid of all the trouble that followed her.

When the waiter stops by to refill our drinks, we see that Marc has already finished his half of the meal and we cave in. Jon asks if he wants another one. "If it's okay," says Marc.

"You can have that," Leah says, pointing to her half of the food.

"No, no, no," Marc says, "that's your dinner."

"No, you can have it."

"I've already ordered another one," he says. Leah shrugs and goes on.

Her public speaking also alienated her friends, her mother, and one of her daughters, she says. Like "Seth," "Leah Haley" is a pseudonym, adopted to protect her family from the inevitable attention that her public speaking brings.

"I'm very proud of her for speaking up about this, because she lost so much," says Marc. "You wouldn't believe the kind of house she lived in. She lost her first husband, she lost her job, one of her daughters won't speak to her, her mother thinks she's consorting with demons, and—,"

"My car," she says wistfully.

"She lost her car."

"That's my hardest thing. I had a Honda Accord. I loved my Honda Accord."

"We can't afford two cars anymore," Marc says.

Leah lost everything in the divorce (her daughters were grown, fortunately, so custody wasn't an issue), and after such a bitter experience, she was in no hurry to get hitched again. During the course of her speaking work and research, she became more involved with people in the UFO field and eventually ran into Marc at a UFO conference.

"You guys need to go to a UFO conference," he says. "Have you been to a conference? When you go to a UFO conference, what happens is you find that you have *come home.* It's like a huge family reunion. These people, they're all outcasts in their own communities because of their beliefs. But when they go to these conferences, they all feel like they're together and like they can talk about whatever they want to and they feel like they're at home. And you can feel the energy from those people."

Amid all of this energy and community spirit, Leah and Marc finally noticed each other. "We fought against it, but we were unable to prevent it," he says. "Can you imagine marrying someone that you've never dated?" At the time they met, Marc was already happily married. (I can see the tabloid headline now: "ALIEN WIFE-SWAPPERS!")

"When we got together," Leah says, "we had seen each other at conferences four times, and all of our communication was business. Then all of a sudden I started having these messages put in my head from some outside force. It was really weird." Marc and his wife divorced and then he and Leah got married and went into business together.

Greenleaf grew out of their experiences at the UFO conferences. After Leah gave a lecture, people would say how they wished that they could buy books on the subject, but that their bookstore didn't carry them. Leah and Marc thought it would be helpful to bring all of those books together in one place, and soon they were setting up their mail-order business.

"We have gone totally head over heels into debt," says Leah, "borrowing through the nose to try to build up a publishing company and mail-order company, selling books of this nature to try to educate the public about this subject." Leah handles the finances, writes the blurbs in the catalog, and takes the orders. Marc is stuck with most of the grunt work involved in packaging and shipping books. "So we work, all the time," she says. "Seven days a week, really. From the time we get up in the morning until the time we go to bed at night. If we weren't interviewing with you guys tonight we'd still be working." Not a total waste of their valuable time, I suppose, since they got the dinner they wanted.

"The profit margin's not very high," she continues. "So—we don't make much."

Our waiter delivers Marc's meal, and Marc turns to Leah, pointing his fork at her plate. "Eat this before it gets cold," he says.

"I'm okay," she says. "I'm okay."

I ask if they're on the Internet. Leah nods yes, but doesn't seem too excited. "People who surf the Internet, surf the Internet," says Marc. "They apparently don't read books. They're busy reading something off the Internet. They come to our Web site, they look at the pages, it looks good, then they move on. Most of the people on there don't have time to read books." He shrugs. "We sell very few books that way."

The business sounds like a nightmare to me. And as much as I appreciate the struggling artist lifestyle, I fully intend to get a day job while I write this book. Why doesn't Leah just get another accounting job?

"I can get another accounting job anytime I want to," she says confidently. "I have an MBA and plenty of experience. The reason I'm doing this is because I believe in it. I know how it affected me." In essence, she's not just doing a job—she's on a mission, following a calling.

"If the public were adequately educated about the reality of the phenomenon," Leah says, "then no one ever again would have to lose a spouse. No one ever again would have to lose a job. If everybody knew what was going on, there would be no reason for anybody to ever go through what I've had to go through. A lot of people live through this life, they live and die, and all they do is take, they don't give anything. I'd like to think that I've helped somebody. So if I could die helping one other person not have to go through what I've gone through—that's why I got involved with what I'm doing now."

In addition to writing and selling books, Leah has also made appearances on radio and television programs, including *The Joan Rivers Show*. As somebody who's paying his own way across the country, I wonder how those deals work for her. Does she pay her own travel expenses? "God—Hell—no," blurts Leah, shaking her head. "We can't even afford to pay the rent, much less hotel expenses. No."

"She really doesn't like to do interviews," Marc says, "but she does them because she feels it's necessary."

For as annoying as it's been for her to foist her husband on us (and our wallets), I grant that Leah has been an extremely talkative, open person. I tell her I had been expecting more caution, more distance. Something closer to how Bruce and Ann Morrison behaved in Gulf Breeze, instead of the way she shares details of not only her abduction experiences but also her personal life (although I suppose few things can be more personal and embarrassing than an abduction). "Well, I don't have anything to hide," she says. "As far as I'm concerned, what else have I got to lose? I mean, I've lost everything already." She laughs, one tinged by hysteria or desperation, then repeats, quietly, "So what have I got to lose?"

Leah has been burned by people in her private life—friends, family, co-workers—on account of her speaking out about her abduction experiences, but for the most part, she says, the media have been very kind to her. Journalists have generally treated her with respect and compassion. The local newspaper ran a two-page spread on the UFO interest group that Leah and Marc started up last year, and the local radio station has asked them to come on the air countless times, giving them "free rein" of the studio.

But media exposure also opens them to attack. "There has been the occasional caller who would say, 'Well, I don't believe you. You just made up this story so you could write books and make a lot of money,'" Leah says, laughing in disbelief. Authorship has had the opposite sort of effect on Leah. She holds up a copy of *Ceto's New Friends,* a slim hardcover book with a colorful, glossy cover. "This book costs me $7.79—*per book*—to produce," she says. "My distributor pays me $6.25 a book for the books the distributor sells. But it was so important to me that kids learn about the existence of aliens that I'm willing to spare it." Leah makes a profit on the few copies she sells through Greenleaf, breaking about even in the end. "But people who don't have any better sense think that just because you write a book you automatically become a millionaire," she says. "It really hurts when I get comments like that, and I don't know how I'm going to pay my rent next month."

At least the rent in Murfreesboro can't be that painful. Being writers and mail-order business people, Leah and

Marc could have set up shop anywhere in the country. They drove from Mississippi to California looking for the right place to settle, finally choosing Murfreesboro for reasons that they haven't quite figured out themselves.

"I think we were needed here," proposes Leah. "We started up a UFO interest group here, we just started it up last summer, and we already have more than a hundred members, who were *starving* for information."

"Everybody that we've met—," adds Marc, "like our real estate agent, the people that cut your hair, all the people, they ask us what we do, and we tell them and they say, 'Oh, well, we had a sighting,' and then their neighbor doesn't know it."

"Or they would say to us, 'We've been *dying* to tell somebody this, but we don't want to tell anybody in Murfreesboro because they'll think we're crazy,'" Leah says. "So you've got this coming from the banker, you've got it coming from the real estate agent, you've got it coming from the printer, you've got it coming from all these people. So, we had a whole town full of people here who have had sightings—but they're scared to tell each other."

"But there's another reason, too," Marc says.

Leah nods. "There's a practical reason, too."

"After we moved here, and we started selling books of all kinds," says Marc, "we found out that we're 17 miles from the world's largest supplier of books—Ingram. Ingram is a distributor right up the street here in La Vergne."

"And we didn't have a clue."

Despite the low profits they're pulling in, Leah feels

she's well-suited to her duties at Greenleaf. "I have the grammar and punctuation English skills to be a writer and I have the accounting skills and the management skills to run the business," she notes. "So it all has worked out very nicely."

She speaks of being "told" to marry Marc, she doesn't know why she moved to Murfreesboro, and she has said that aliens have been "teaching" her things that she can't recall in conscious detail. Does she think it was by design that things worked out so well with her job?

"*He* does," she says, smirking and glancing sideways at Marc. "I don't know. I'm the skeptic."

Marc says that he's examined so many abductees' histories—including his own, for he may be one—that he's come to the conclusion that everything that happens in their lives trains them for the jobs that they've chosen. "They've been prepared for the job that they're doing now," he says, "including—and this is another can of worms to open this late, but—including the fact that they're brought together with their mates to be able to continue doing this kind of work, whereas most mates like her first husband wouldn't put up with it. It appears that people are prepared specifically to do jobs like educating the public about this." He believes that aliens are not only abducting people, but programming and directing their lives.

"Talking about the preparation—this is the one thing that's scary," says Leah. "And I sure didn't mean to go into this much. But the one thing that's scary, though, is some of the things that we have been prepared to do." One central aspect of the abduction experience is that the subjects are given messages about preserving the earth's environment as well as visions of an apocalyptic future. "Talking about these earth changes—when I was growing up, I had to help my mother grow foods in the garden, I had to help prepare the foods, I had to help freeze, I had to help can. I had to do all that stuff, so I know that I can dig, and plant a seed, and grow." She motions to Marc, saying, "He was taught how to live off the land even to a *deeper* extent than I was. Really live off the land. And he is really good at making things, designing things, and creating things from scratch and making do with makeshift stuff. And that kind of frightens me, because I think, why were we prepared to do all of these things if we're not going to have to do them? And if these predictions that all of these abductees have been given come true, then we're probably going to be better able to survive than a lot of people because we have training in working off the land."

His plate clean once again, Marc turns to Leah, who has hardly touched hers. "Eat your dinner," he says.

"I've had all I want," she replies.

"You have?"

"I had plenty," she assures Marc, pushing the plate over to him. He starts to polish off the last of it. "Did you already have lunch today?" she asks. "You didn't have lunch, did you?"

"No," Marc admits.

Leah shakes her head. "No wonder you're starving."

"That's too bad," says Jon, eyeing the plate. "I had a question for Marc, but now he's eating ..."

Marc laughs, telling him to go right ahead, and Jon asks about the specifics of the coming apocalypse. Marc says that after the predicted disaster, such as a meteor strike or a pole shift (however that would be accomplished), most of the population will die. Those who are left will be thrown back into the Stone Age and will have to fend for themselves. "They'll have to grow their own food, forage for food, they'll have to teach all of the people from then on, everything," he says. "From mathematics to government, everything."

"And that's another thing that's scary, see," Leah says nervously. "I have the training in math, I have the training in English, and grammar, and all that stuff, and he's a scientist. So, you know, these things cross our minds every once in a while. And then sometimes I think, 'Garbage! You're mind's just running wild.'"

"But you'd be surprised how many people have been compelled to move out of the cities," says Marc, "because the cities obviously will crumble during a time like this. It's generally thought that the people who are pretty much worthless, the people who are now basically leeching off the rest of society—the bank robbers and the drug users and all those people—will perish. And it's generally thought that the people who will be saved are those who are out in the countryside working hard to sustain themselves." I wonder which category Jon and I fall into, traveling through the countryside at a grueling pace, yet for no practical purpose, and what category Marc falls into, parlaying his wife's abduction experience into a free dinner.

"It's being taught to an awful lot of people," he goes on,

"and if it's not true, my question is, Why in the *heck* are they going to so much trouble to teach it to so many people? All over the world! Not just here, but everywhere."

His final hypothesis, then, is that the aliens, whoever they are, feel that humanity—despite its behavior, despite pollution and war and everything else—has something worth salvaging. "They're trying to ensure that what is left after this coming cataclysm is not only just nature but also humanity."

Jerking a thumb at herself, Leah says, "And then skeptic over here sits and thinks, 'Well, yeah, all that's a possibility, but then what if it's just somebody up there with a sadistic sense of humor?'"

"So she's still trying to set up an IRA so we'll have something …," Marc says, and everyone laughs.

"Well," says Jon, "it sounds like you've got all the options covered."

"Let me tell you something about her that she won't say about herself," Marc says as we're winding up dinner, sorting out the checks (Jon picks up both, garnering thanks from Marc). "She's a CPA. She has two master's degrees—one in education and one in business administration. When debunkers say, 'Well, why doesn't this happen to someone who's educated?'—well, it *does*. It happens to doctors, lawyers, physicians, government leaders, and CPAs and everybody else. And not only is she articulate and educated, but she is highly skeptical herself. She was the last person to accept this. It's not like someone wide-eyed—someone who believes anything that comes along. That's not her."

Out at their van, Leah and Marc give us a copy of their catalog. I guess we don't rate high enough for review copies of books, though, because we're forced to pay $50 for *Ceto's New Friends, Lost Was the Key,* and *Visitors from Time,* the three titles we really need to understand these people. As I write them a check, Marc jokes, "I didn't know we were going to sell books tonight!"

Jon is fairly pissed as we return to the car and drive back to the hotel—partly because it was his turn to buy dinner tonight, but mostly because of the condescending way Marc treated us. We agree that Leah was an excellent interview subject, but Marc didn't become co-operative until we agreed to pay. His comment about selling books particularly incenses Jon, since we were roped into spending money tonight.

Was Marc condescending because we're the damned, and therefore don't deserve any respect? Are we two out of the billions who will be killed in the great cataclysm? They, after all, are the elect, chosen and guided by the aliens. All I can say is, nice going, aliens.

A question: How qualified are the aliens? Leah is no writer. When I asked her if she had any previous writing experience before tackling *Lost,* Marc said, "What he wants to know is why it's so well-written." Leah seemed a bit embarrassed at that, looking at us as if her child had just said something incredibly rude but was too young to be aware of it. She used to teach English, so *Lost Was the Key's* grammar and punctuation are impeccable, but I think she knows she's no wordsmith. The book teeters on the verge of being fatally dull. She took the exciting and compelling story of a woman discovering a life she never knew she was leading, whose world was turned upside-down, whose views of reality were forever altered, and she sucked the energy out of it. It's flat and prosaic, the dialogue stumbles, and there's no attempt to set any sorts of scenes—it's just a journal of the events, lacking in deep insight or reflection, that's been translated into book form. If the aliens are choosing people to spread the word, why are their communicators so poor, or, like Marc, so annoying? His behavior effectively sabotaged Leah's attempt to spread the word tonight, and turned Jon off completely. And, if he's so driven, so selfless about his mission, why is he so hung up on the copyright of *Dear Mr. President?*

What would compel a CPA to pursue an unprofitable career of writing and bookselling? Marc's right on one point: Leah doesn't seem the gullible type, and she's not crazy, though she initially prayed that she was, since it would have meant that her condition could be treated and cured. But it cannot. She's not crazy. We've met crazy people—people like Earl in Gulf Breeze, whom even the UFO believers laughed at. But when you meet Leah, she's not wacky or irrational. She's a perfectly reasonable human being—a little mousy maybe, but that's to be expected after what she's been through. Once pressed, she's shockingly honest. And most important, Leah is skeptical, and the first to admit how crazy everything in her life seems. But she's not crazy.

Is she stupid? She has two master's degrees, but

she's working in shipping, barely scraping out a living. Why not take an accounting job and use the money to run Greenleaf on the side, to hire someone else to do the grunt work?

Maybe she feels that, if she doesn't do it, no one else will. She told us that she felt the need to educate the public so that no one else would have to go through what she did, to lose what she did, all because she and the people in her life didn't understand what was going on. It seems that, as much as she complains about the pressures of work and money, she loves her work, and needs to do it.

Jon and I unwind in the hotel room, bitching about dinner, about our own lack of money, and about the weeks of excruciating driving that lay ahead. We don't even know if our stories will ever be published, or if we'll ever recoup these costs, ever be compensated for tonight's $90 tab, but the whole project seems like something we should do; something that, in the end, despite all the hassle, we actually enjoy.

Maybe Leah is just as stupid as we are.

UFOs for Elvis

Memphis, Tennessee
May 31, 1996
J.F.

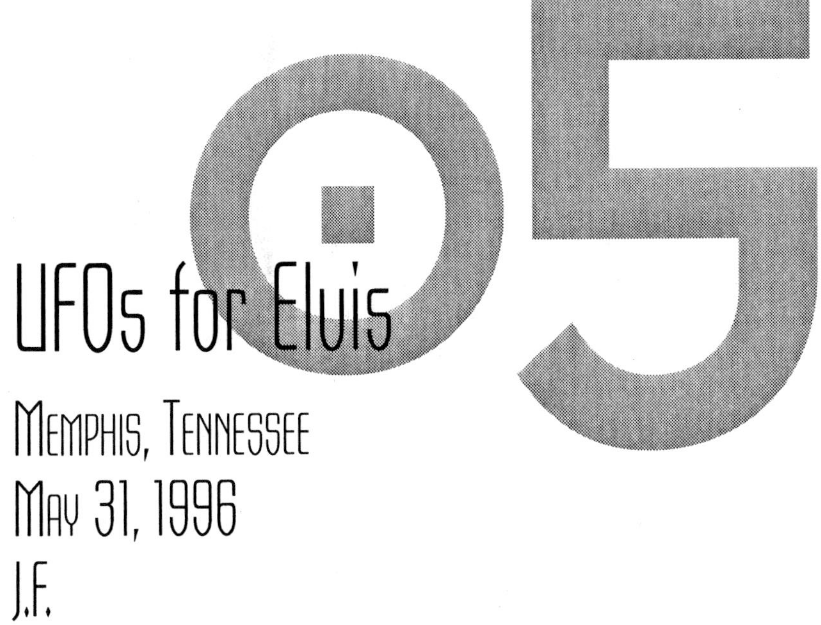

att and I arrive at Graceland just in time to catch one of the last tours of the afternoon. Tickets for the excursion are sold across the street from the King's home at a complex that includes a gift shop and restaurant. Apparently, the Presley family wants to keep commercialism at least 100 yards away from Elvis's legacy and final resting place; close enough to see, but not close enough to corrupt. We buy two tickets and are about to board the tour bus when Matt notices a sign warning that no video recording equipment will be allowed on the premises. There are bus-terminal-style storage lockers nearby, and we rush to find one for the Hi-8. This is the first time we've been prohibited from videotaping a location we've visited on our journey, and leaving the camera behind gives me

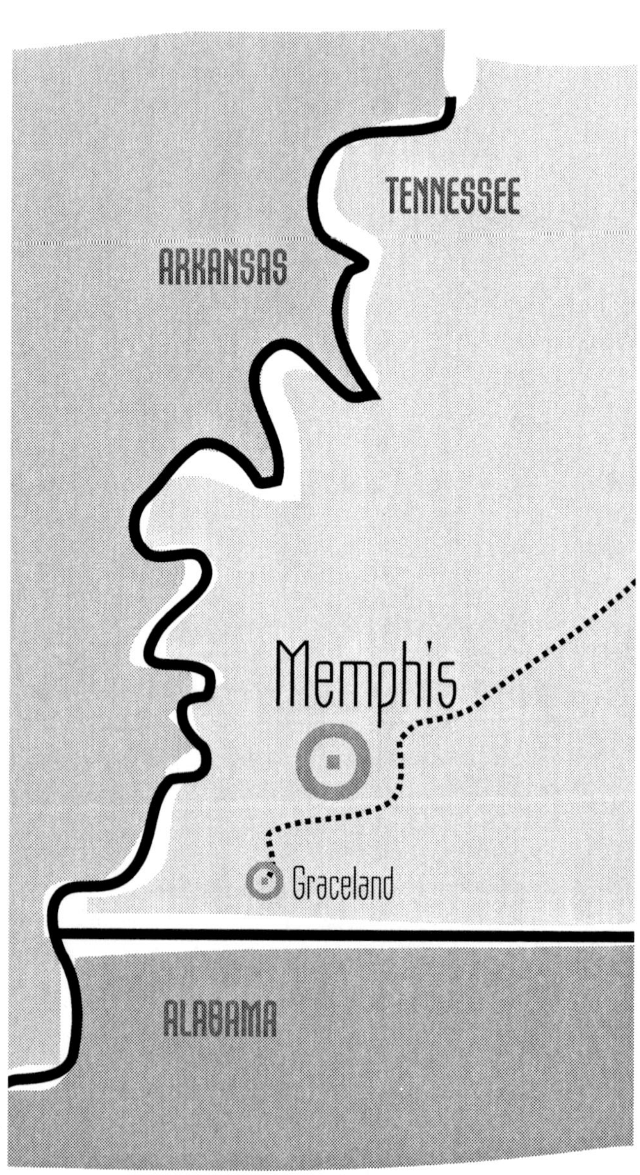
TENNESSEE
ARKANSAS
Memphis
Graceland
ALABAMA

a strange, incongruous feeling. Our ability to document our adventure here has been reduced significantly. Matt is equally irritated, but, in the name of getting the job done, he deposits two quarters into the coin slot and grabs the locker key.

The people standing before the accordion-like bus door are dwindling in number, and we hurry so we won't miss our ride. A Graceland employee standing at the head of the line hands me my personal tour guide—a cassette tape, tape player, and headphones. Apparently, tapes are more efficient than humans, who mix up their facts, call in sick, and bill overtime.

As I sit waiting for the bus to leave, I ponder the reasons Matt and I have come to Graceland. Elvis and UFOs are the two big tabloid newspaper staples of the '90s. If a celebrity mom isn't beating her kids this week or a rock star isn't overdosing on heroin, the gossip rags run the

Get you tickets and stow your video cameras here.

tried and true, Elvis and UFOs. The only thing better than one of these is both; You can't miss the "Elvis Abducted by Space Fiends" or the "Elvis Still Alive on Venus" headlines that glut the supermarket check-out counters. But why have both Elvis and the UFO phenomenon grabbed so tightly ahold of the American imagination?

The bus rolls lazily across Elvis Presley Boulevard to the front entrance of the King's estate. The wrought-iron gates swing open, and the vehicle chugs up the curved driveway, past wide expanses of carefully cut grass. Graceland is a two-story stone mansion with a beautiful Southern-style front porch. Tall, white Greek columns support the porch roof, and a pair of stone lions guard the steps. Given all the security so far, I'm certain there are sharpshooters watching from the upper windows.

We disembark from the bus and enter the building. Once inside, the tour tape leads us from room to room, offering Elvis anecdotes, snippets of his music, and brief histories of the sights we're viewing. Elvis's elaborate dining room comes complete with a giant crystal chandelier and place settings for nonexistent guests. The garishly decorated Jungle Room, assembled for the King's amusement, features an intricately carved wood throne and footstool, both upholstered with brown-and-black-striped fur. In Elvis's entertainment room downstairs, three televisions glare at us from their perches in the back wall.

Matt snaps pictures with his 35mm camera. No sooner does the shutter click than we are reminded by the minimal security staff that these pictures are for private use only, and explicit permission from Elvis's estate must be given in order for them to be used otherwise. I feel the controlling hand of Big Brother tightening his grip around my throat, and I wonder what the King would have to say on the matter.

May 25, 1998

Matthew M. Holm
▆▆▆▆▆▆▆▆▆▆
7th Floor
New York, NY 10019

Dear Matthew,

Thank you for contacting us regarding photo use in your forthcoming book *Gray Highway: An American UFO Journey*. Although the premise of your book sounds interesting, we do not feel comfortable in becoming formally involved in a UFO story line. Therefore, we are unable to grant permission for you to use photos of Graceland or Elvis in your book. However, we do wish you luck in your publishing endeavor.

Sincerely,

Todd Andersen
Creative Resources Assistant

Graceland, Division of Elvis Presley Enterprises, Inc.
3734 Elvis Presley Boulevard, Memphis, Tennessee 38116/901-332-3322

Why all of our photos are from outside of Graceland

DOWN AT THE END OF LONELY STREET

DOWN AT THE

END OF

LONELY STREET

960531

Part of the house has been converted into a museum which displays row after row of Presley's gold and platinum singles; posters from his movies; his costumes, including his rhinestone-encrusted cape; his army and karate uniforms; and his guns. There are also exhibits highlighting Elvis's charitable efforts. In these rooms and throughout the mansion, I can see the reasons why an entire nation adored the King, and why aliens might want to abduct him.

Great musical talent attracts and amazes people; it stretches their imaginations, allows them to dream, and makes them feel as if they're part of something bigger. No one knows where such ability originates, and in that respect, fantastic talent is simply a miracle.

What else could possibly explain how a poor white Southern boy could croon his way into the heart of the world? To his many followers, Elvis wasn't just a man, but a hero, worthy of admiration and maybe even worship. The most fervent of Elvis's fans still can't believe he's gone. It's no wonder so many tabloids proclaim that "Elvis Is Alive."

Like Elvis's musical gift, the UFO phenomenon is loaded with what pundits construe to be modern-day miracles. Lights in the sky and alien abductions are the seeds of what could someday become a religion. Perhaps UFOlogy already is. Whatever the reasons behind the Elvis shrines in suburban homes and the UFO fever which Matt and I seem to have willingly caught, this much is true: These things add meaning to people's lives.

Elvis's well-tended grave lies out behind the mansion, near fountains and a kidney-shaped swimming pool.

Fresh flowers and tiny American flags have been placed around the King's tomb. And, at the bottom of the inscription remembering Elvis Aaron Presley is his "Taking Care of Business in a Flash" insignia.

We board the bus and return to the visitors' center complex. At the gift shop, I buy two Elvis pens and several Elvis postcards. We retrieve the Hi-8 from the locker. It's been a long day and we're hungry, so we check out the diner next door. Unfortunately for us, The King's Heartbreak Hotel Restaurant is closed.

A Pig, a Giant Cow, & a Mutilated Wallet

We're on our way to Roswell, N.Mex., via U.S. Route 60. The highway speed limit is 65 MPH, and I'm cruising at a conservative 70 MPH. I can smell the gaggingly sweet odor of manure in the air. To add to my discomfort, my stomach keeps reminding me it's lunch time in a series of grunts and gurgles. I listen to the radio, try to ignore the stench that's seeping in through what's supposed to be the fresh air vents, and generally pay little attention to the vast expanses of dull browns and pale greens zipping by the car. It's not very exciting driving.

My ruined senses are barely functional enough to register the police cruiser as we pass it. A split second later, I'm paying full attention to the road again. My heart freezes solid, and I slam on the brakes. I glance fearfully from the

Amarillo
Bovina
NEW MEXICO
TEXAS

MONTANA
New Salem
NORTH DAKOTA
SOUTH DAKOTA

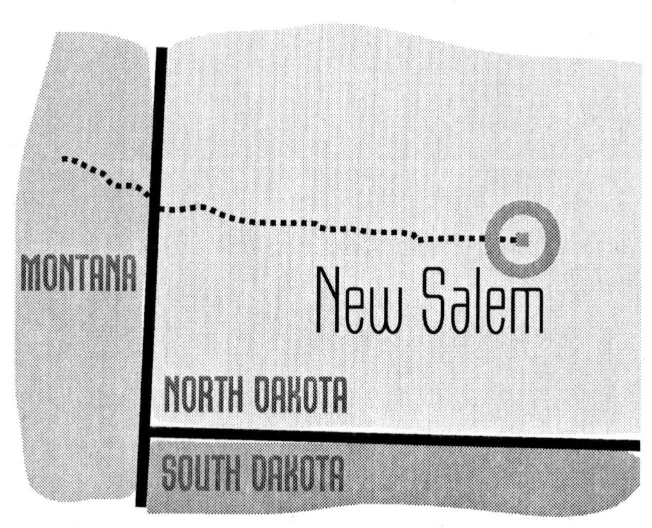

speedometer to the 45-MPH speed limit sign to the speedometer again. Forty-five MPH? How'd we get in a 45-MPH zone? The blue and red lights on the cruiser come to life, flashing wildly. Apparently, Matt and I have entered Bovina without even knowing it.

"Damn! Damn! Damn!" I curse under my breath. I slow down and pull into the parking lot of a nearby gas station.

The police officer is a young guy with a thick Texas accent. I can't tell if he likes his job very much, but he's on the ball, at any rate. I hand him my license and the Geo's registration. As he wanders back to the cruiser, I contemplate the perfection of the Bovina speed trap. Placed like an afterthought near the Texas–New Mexico border, the town is a short strip of gas stations, grain elevators, warehouses, and other odds and ends of buildings, located in the middle of U.S. Route 60. Without a magnifying glass, it's impossible to separate Bovina from the barren wasteland that surrounds it. As you enter town, the speed limit changes from 65 MPH to 45 MPH in a matter of yards. All that a policeman looking for an easy score has to do is wait by the roadside until an unobservant driver, like myself, comes along.

The cop returns with a pre-printed, we-know-you-don't-live-here-so-here's-how-to-mail-us-the-money instruction sheet. Apparently, Bovina makes a good deal of cash from out-of-towners. He clocked me doing 55 MPH in a 45 MPH zone and, according to the worksheet, the fine is $60. In a matter of minutes, I have provided him with a day's wages. He bids us

Working for $360 an hour

good-bye and advises us to drive safely.

Since we have already stopped, Matt and I decide we might as well have our lunch. As we're taking the food out of the cooler, the cop returns to the parking lot with another hapless victim. I sip a Coke and calculate that it took him a total of ten minutes to take care of us, from start to finish. At this rate, if he was working hard, he'd have 6 customers in the next hour, making an easy $360 for the town of Bovina, assuming everyone paid the fine. What a beautiful scam. Matt and I decide that the policeman's extortion post is no place to enjoy our lunch, so we get back in the car and leave, but not before I videotape him and his next customer.

The strangeness isn't over yet. In fact, it's just beginning. As we drive away, I see that the notice board by the gas station reads, "WAY TO GO HAYLEE CLASS OF 2008." Being that it's 1996, the class of 2008 has just finished kindergarten. Barely out of diapers, it's unlikely that the little tykes can read the sign, making the board either a point of pride for their parents or a sinister message that outsiders aren't meant to understand. There's something not right about this town; that's for sure.

Farther down U.S. Route 60, we come upon Bovina's namesake and the source of the pungent smell that assailed our nostrils earlier. At first, we can't believe our eyes. By the side of the road are acres upon acres of tightly packed cattle, a sea of beef, mooing unhappily. In Bovina, there are, no doubt, significantly more cows than people.

Popular UFO lore is filled with tales of cattle mutilation. These stories purport that aliens suck the cow completely dry of blood, coring out the anus, genitalia, and eyes. All the cuts are incredibly precise, made with a laser-like instrument. Supposedly, aliens extract vital enzymes from the cow parts to supplement their feeble digestive systems, leaving frightened farmers to wonder. So they say.

A sign of the future

Beyond the miles of cattle, Matt and I stop at a picnic area to eat the remainder of our lunch. Maybe, I suggest, the U.S. government is trying to stop us from finding out the truth in Bovina. Haylee Class of 2008? What's that about? Is it an announcement of the long-anticipated extraterrestrial arrival? And perhaps the speeding ticket is a scare tactic to warn us away from the underground alien base and the cattle corpses. Or, maybe I was just driving too fast.

We finish our sandwiches, agreeing that the true answer will remain forever a mystery, buried deep in the brain of a hick-town cop. It would be better for us, we conclude, if we didn't ask any more questions. Putting the cattle conspiracy behind us, we drive away from Bovina, at a perfectly legal speed.

Jump ahead three weeks. It's June 21, 1996, and Matt and I are beginning to wonder if there is some truth to the theory that cattle attract UFOs. This hypothesis is weighing heavily on our minds when we see a giant cow slowly rise in the light of the setting sun. We've arrived in New Salem, N.Dak.

Her name is Salem Sue, and she stands on a hill overlooking the highway. Sue is 38 feet high and 50 feet nose to tail; long wires are pulled taut to the ground by her side to support her huge frame. I stare up at her, admiring all 12,000 pounds of her bovine magnificence. According to the bronze plaque by her base, Sue was built in 1974 with $40,000 contributed by the apparently insane New Salem dairy community. The plaque goes on to explain that she is still maintained by the New Salem Lions Club, the authors and organizers of her creation. It doesn't take much to see that something is dreadfully wrong with this town. It's infected with the same strangeness as Bovina. I keep a sharp eye out for aliens and policemen.

As we stand beneath Sue's black-and-white stomach, I finally give in to temptation, grabbing one of the giant teats that descend like stalactites from her five-foot-wide udder. On the way back to the road, we encounter another sign that reads "FOR COW UPKEEP, THANKS!" The soliciting sign is accompanied by a little box with a white arrow pointing to a notch in the top of it. They'll get no cash from us. We're against mad civil engineering projects.

Before we get back into the Geo, I gaze over the seemingly endless fields of grass that surround Salem Sue and the stretch of empty highway that will lead us back East. I wonder, absently, why the hell anyone in his right mind

Ground zero for the ultimate in cattle mutilation

The cow sets in the West.

would bother to build this bovine monstrosity here, in the middle of nowhere. As I try to fathom an answer, my thoughts are filled with visions of circling UFOs. The spacecraft are sending down bursts of light to transport Sue up to the heavens. Then again, I think, who am I to determine who's in his right mind? Perhaps the New Salemers aren't so goofy after all.

Terrestrial Tourism

Roswell, New Mexico
June 4, 1996
J.F.

The land that surrounds Roswell is brown, barren, and flat—the perfect place for a three-point UFO landing, if you had a UFO to land. Thin clouds sit low in the New Mexican sky, distant hills sigh purple-black, and gaudy signs litter the roadside. As Matt and I reach the city limits, a billboard advertising a local car dealership reminds us that "THE FUTURE IS BRIGHT IN ROSWELL." We, however, are less interested in the future of this town than we are in its past.

In early July, 1947, Mac Brazel, a rancher from Lincoln County, N.Mex., found some strange, metallic debris strewn across a field near his home. Unable to identify the type of metal of which the pieces were constructed and baffled as to how they had arrived there, Brazel collected a few of the smaller bits and showed them to his neigh-

gray·highway

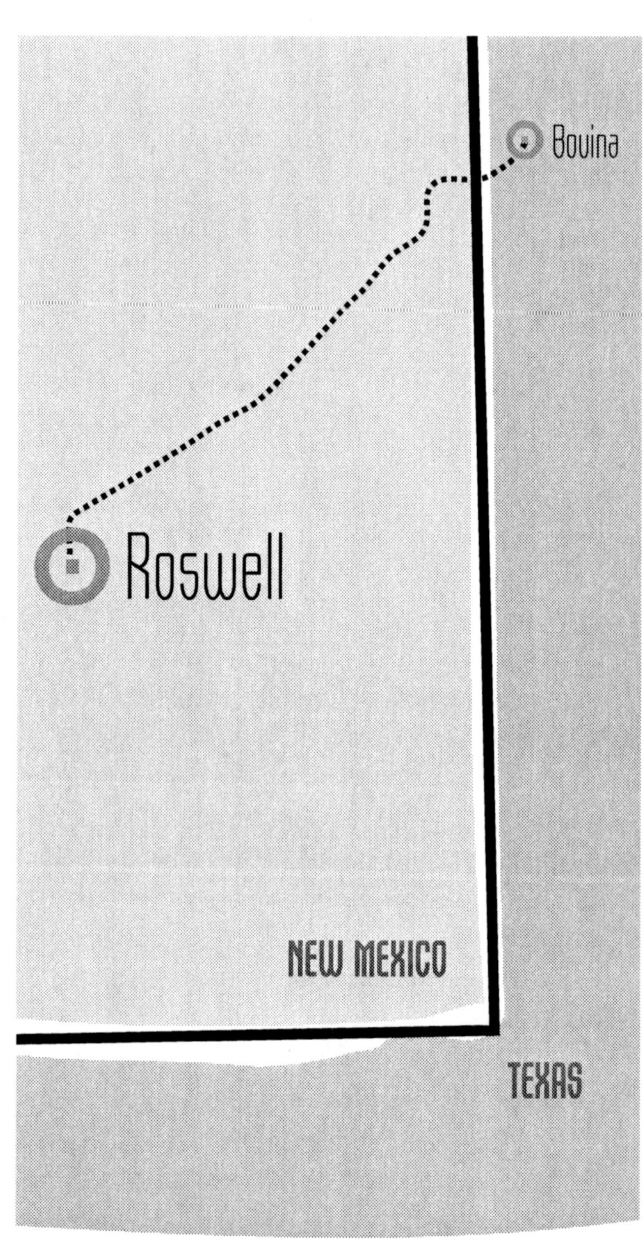
Bovina
Roswell
NEW MEXICO
TEXAS

bors, Floyd and Loretta Proctor. They didn't recognize the substance either, so Brazel decided to bring the debris samples to the town of Roswell and Sheriff George Wilcox. Wilcox examined Brazel's find and contacted the Roswell Army Air Field, which immediately sent an investigation team. From there, everything went straight to hell. Brazel was detained by the military and interrogated. Every last piece of the debris was collected from the field and shipped off to be analyzed while the press was officially told that the crashed object was only a weather balloon.

Since then, a host of UFO investigators have asked the question: If the debris came from a common weather balloon, why was such secrecy necessary? Speculation regarding the incident has grown to include a host of theories, the most fascinating postulating that the recovered debris was part of an alien ship and that the U.S. military, in addition to seizing the wreckage, also whisked away

Entering Roswell

the bodies of the UFO's extraterrestrial pilots, supposedly found at a nearby site. An answer to the Roswell question, following this particular paradigm, is one that could alter human understanding forever, which is why the pursuit of new evidence still continues almost 50 years later. Whatever the truth may be, it's unlikely that the Roswell puzzle will ever be solved, making the town's resulting tourist industry easier to understand. Roswell is a mystery, and everyone loves a mystery.

When Matt and I arrive in town, we are bombarded by a media blitz announcing the upcoming Roswell UFO Encounters '96. Unfortunately, we're a month early for the festivities and must be satisfied imagining such events as the UFO Crash & Burn Expo, a "non-motorized alien space craft parade competition," and the Moon-Walk 4-Man Golf Tourney, a nighttime golf tournament where players tee off with glow-in-the-dark balls. The mascot for Roswell UFO Encounters is a cartoon alien with a melon-shaped head and four suction-cup fingers on each hand who cruises across the universe in a bathtub-like space mobile. Press for the Crash & Burn Expo declares "The '95 UFO float race was the most photographed and widely publicized event at that '95 UFO Encounter. It was covered by local, state and national media." Obviously, corporate sponsors should give this highly visible event a look—at $100 per entry, of course.

Clearly, the UFO crash—real or imagined—has provided Roswell with a tangible national identity, defining it in a way that sports, music, or industry defines other cities: When people think Roswell, they think UFOs. Most interesting is that the Roswell community has willingly aligned itself with an event that is equal parts historical event and unsolved mystery. The missing debris from an alien spacecraft holds as much weight here as the Statue of Liberty does in New York City or the Freedom Trail does in Boston.

UFOs are a big draw in Roswell, which supports two museums and a number of other services dedicated to the 1947 incident. Matt and I first stop at the UFO Enigma Museum, housed in a lonely, one-story building attached to a row of warehouses on the edge of town. Admission is a mere $1.

Enigma's exhibits aren't exactly fit for the Smithsonian, but the information they contain is intriguing. One display features a collection of front-page newspaper articles that appeared in *The Roswell Daily Record* during that fateful week in 1947. Headlines such as "RAAF Captures Flying Saucer on Ranch in Roswell Region," and "General Ramey

The Enigma Museum's official wheels

Empties Roswell Saucer," are stamped across yellowing paper. A more recent issue of *The Roswell Daily Record*, dated 1991, has a picture of three ultra-serious-looking men in suits sitting at a table with the header "UFO Day Proclaimed." Even if the aliens never came to Roswell, it's clear they'll never leave.

Enigma's life-size exhibit of the crash site is campy, spaceman kitsch. Smiling, stuffed Gray dolls, disturbingly similar to the ones you can buy in the Enigma gift shop, lie in awkward positions on the ground around a poorly painted UFO. Desert animals freeze in bizarre poses as a mannequin made to look like a Military Police officer surveys the scene. I take a peek inside the video viewing room to see a bored-looking tourist family of four reclining on white patio chairs, glazed eyes staring at a UFO documentary.

Enigma's curator, John Price, is a tough-looking, bearded man, wearing jeans and a long-sleeve shirt with Native American prints. John talks with us easily and is willing to be videotaped. "I believe in the UFO phenomenon," he says. "If you follow the document trail and the good eyewitness testimony and disregard so much of the junk we've been fed over the last 50 years through films and tabloids, you'll find that there are a lot of credible people out there. I know people in my family and outside of my family who have had sightings that have never been explained." John, however, has not seen any lights in the sky himself. "There's something out there that we're not being told the truth about, and my views and research lead me to believe it's extraterrestrials," John says.

Running the UFO Enigma museum has fulfilled Price's boyhood dream. "It came to a point around 1987 when I felt that locally somebody should do something to get people to look at the incident a little more seriously. We started in 1988 putting up a few displays in our local business. From there we evolved into a museum." For John, the search to understand the UFO phenomenon is not just a way to earn a living, it's a lifetime goal.

John Price, proprietor of the UFO Enigma Museum

The International UFO Museum and Research Center

Matt and I next visit the International UFO Museum and Research Center, which is located in the center of town. The IUFOM is more slickly produced than Enigma. The exterior signs, the brochures, and even the crash-landed UFO embedded above the doorway have a professional sheen. The IUFOM is staffed entirely by volunteers and admission is free. As we enter the building, the woman at the front desk protests the Hi-8 camera that Matt's toting. We have to obtain special permission to get in the door with it.

The mismatched competition between Roswell's two UFO museums is difficult to ignore. Here at the IUFOM, the mood is much more serious. Free-standing displays and well-crafted exhibits fill the main room, a far cry from Enigma's haphazard construction. Exhibits containing newspaper clips, photographs, models, and drawings are neatly placed on the walls. The IUFOM also has several pieces of interesting alien art including a silver and black portrait of five Grays, entitled *We Are Five of Them*, by Marcus Tray, and a surreal UFO crash mural by Miller Johnson. The only truly disappointing exhibit is an "alien autopsy" display from the movie *Roswell* in which a pinkish extraterrestrial lies on a gurney with a curiously attired surgeon waiting nearby. The home-improvement dust mask on the surgeon and the general lack of attention to detail make the whole display seem like a farce, not unlike the crash site exhibit at Enigma. Unfortunately, everyone in Roswell, it seems, needs a draw for the tourism dollars.

After about twenty minutes of filming, Matt informs me that the batteries are running low and that someone will have to sit and guard the camera while they recharge. I find a wall plug in an empty room and prepare myself for a long, dull wait as Matt wanders off to investigate the IUFOM library.

I am only alone for a few moments when Frank, one of the museum volunteers, sits down next to me. Frank is a clean-cut old fellow who is also apparently bored out of his mind and desperate for someone with whom to talk. I ask Frank if he's had a UFO experience. He has.

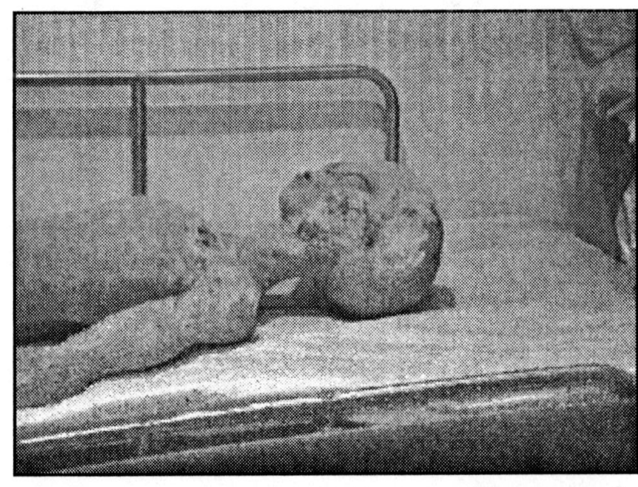

Alien autopsy?

mural at the

international

ufo

museum

mural at the

international

ufo

museum

Viewing exhibits at the International UFO Museum

According to Frank, while he was working on the Los Alamos Air Force Base ground crew, a radar operator spotted a fast-moving blip on the screen, clocking its speed in excess of 5,000 miles per hour. Because of this, Los Alamos was kept on red alert for two days with six planes in rotation and four planes constantly in the air. Whenever two of the planes needed to land and refuel, two others would take off to replace them. Frank and the ground crew were kept busy around the clock.

Frank explains that of the four planes in the air, only two were armed with missiles. The other two were outfitted with special cameras, and the pilots were given these instructions: Photograph the object. Don't shoot at it unless you're firing in self-defense. The object can travel at 5,000 miles per hour, and it will tear you apart.

Frank's interest in the IUFOM has stemmed from this event and, no doubt, John Price's encounters with UFO witnesses have similarly affected him. In their own ways, each of these men has steeped himself in the mystery that lives in Roswell. I can see that, for both Frank and John, the hysteria and hype of UFO capitalism is not nearly as important as coming to terms with a 49-year-old event that is still affecting their lives. They live in a community where the people have, for nearly half a century, had to at least consider the notion that something otherworldly and amazing has happened right outside their doors. If they believe the story is true, they can only wonder if such a privilege or curse will come again. It seems clear that the city of Roswell is definitive of the American UFO spectacle in general: a hodge-podge of pseudoscience and skillful marketing covering an underbelly of actual facts and actual people caught in what, for now, is the undefinable.

Somewhere during the day, Matt and I have managed to pick up an orange flyer advertising guided tours of the crash site. The invitation is accompanied by a phone number you can call for reservations, times you can view the site, and a reminder that the tour is only $15 per person. Given our lack of funds, Matt and I decide to skip it and instead try to locate the site ourselves using the maps at the International UFO Museum.

We mark the location and drive out to the desert. On a barren road 30 miles outside Roswell we realize that (1.) It's pretty far to the site, and (2.) There's probably nothing there anyway. So, we settle for a close approximation. We take a hard left onto a dirt road, drive a quarter mile or so, stop, and get out. Here, in the desert near Roswell, we will try to absorb the atmosphere that Mac Brazel saw every day of his life. Here, we will try to imagine what a crew of military men would look like cleaning up space debris. Here we will try to understand the mystery that has fascinated John Price, Frank, and an entire town for

Bud Light

the past 49 years. We dig through the dirt with our bare hands, and Matt finds a Bud Light can. Perhaps, I suggest, the aliens are social drinkers. We consider saving our find as a souvenir of the mysterious Roswell, but decide to leave it in the ground where it belongs. Sometimes strange metal is best left undisturbed.

Aluminum Shelters with No Walls

Bottomless Lakes State Park, New Mexico
June 4, 1996
J.F.

There are aluminum shelters here with no walls. The shelters are composed of flat roofs supported by thick poles, built over concrete slabs. Underneath each one is an aluminum picnic table, which is chained to a heavy screw sunk into the foundation. The shelters are meant for RVs, but one of them will do fine for our tent.

Matt and I are at Bottomless Lakes State Park, N.Mex., where we'll be camping for the night after our visit to Roswell. The land around us is a dissatisfying brown, and the sparse clumps of green offer our eyes only momentary relief from the monotony.

We shoot some footage with the Hi-8 video camera, establishing for our unknown audience the atmosphere of the New Mexican desert. Then we film a comedy skit. I dress up in silver pleather pants, a silver shirt, and a Gray

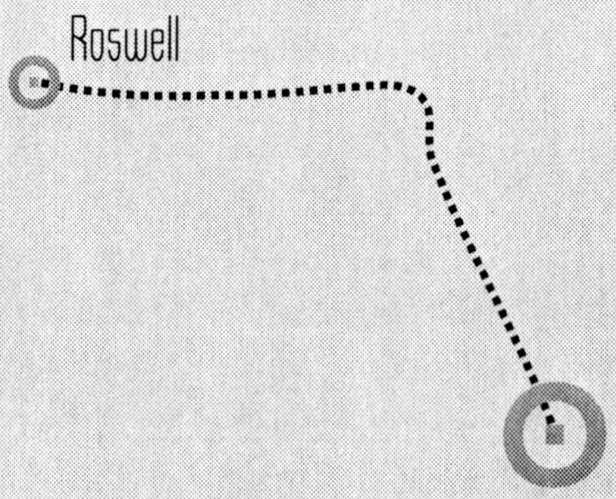

Roswell
Bottomless Lakes S.P.
NEW MEXICO

alien mask and pretend to sneak up on Matt, who stares at the camera, blissfully unaware.

"Two weeks and we haven't seen anything yet. I'm getting a little discouraged. Jon, though, he still thinks there's something out there," Matt says as I leap around behind him trying to get his attention. I wonder if this skit has broader implications for our trip. What are we missing?

We set up camp for the night and cook dinner. There are what seem like millions of bugs swarming around the Coleman stove and gas lamp. They must breed in one of the Bottomless Lakes nearby.

Night falls slowly, like a wounded hand creeping over the desert. As we finish our chili dinner and start cleaning up, I notice a man walking toward our site. His curly brown hair is mostly hidden by his baseball cap, and he looks to be in his early 20s.

"Hey, what's up?" he asks.

"Not much," I say, slightly suspicious. Being on the road has not, in any way, improved my trust of strangers.

"So, what are you guys doing?" he asks.

I look at Matt for guidance. He's much better at repelling unwanted guests than I am. Before either of us can answer, the stranger speaks again. "I heard you talking about aliens."

"Yeah?" Matt replies.

It's clear now that this fellow wants something. "Do you believe they exist?" he asks.

"I'm not really sure," Matt says, trying to give out as little information as possible.

"And we've been to a lot of UFO sites across the country," I say.

"Really? What for?" he asks. I've said the wrong thing. His interest is piqued, and now it's too late to get rid of him.

"We're writing a book about it," I say. A smile crosses his face—not a good sign.

"I'm a writer, too," he says. "Actually, I'm freelancing for a magazine. Do you think I could interview you?"

I look at Matt, who shrugs indifferently.

"Sure," I say. "That's fine."

"I'm Jared, by the way," he says, extending his hand. We shake.

"I'm Jon," I say.

"Matt."

Jared runs back to his campsite, the only other one besides ours in the immediate vicinity.

"This is interesting," I say.

"Eh," Matt replies. He could care less either way. "We attract all the weirdos."

Jared trots back, carrying a notebook in one hand and a pen in the other.

"Hope you don't mind us cleaning up while we talk," I say, gathering up the dishes and heading for the water spigot.

"No, not at all," Jared replies. "So, why are you doing this trip?"

"Well, I guess we're interested in finding out what's going on," I say. "I mean, a lot of Americans believe in UFOs and angels and all that. We want to figure it out for ourselves."

Jared hastily scribbles this down in his notebook.

"How long have you been on the road?" Jared queries.

"What is it now?" I ask Matt, who is packing up the Coleman stove and gas canister.

"Two weeks," Matt says.

"Have you seen anything?" Jared asks Matt.

"Not yet. But, we've run into some strange people," Matt replies.

"What, people who have seen UFOs?" Jared asks.

"Yeah, a few," Matt says. "We talked to an abductee too. She was pretty convincing."

"Do you think it's for real?"

Matt pauses. "Yeah, I think something is happening. I don't know what it is though."

"How about you?" Jared asks me.

"Yeah, something's going on," I reply.

Jared talks to us for another ten minutes or so, before getting his fill.

"You know, when me and my friend Nick heard you talking about UFOs, we wanted to dress up like aliens and try to scare you," Jared says.

"Really? That's great!" Matt says. "Why didn't you do it?"

"We didn't know what we'd use for costumes," Jared says, lamely. "Sheets or something,"—a far cry from silver pleather pants.

Later in the evening, we walk over to Jared and Nick's campsite. They're driving cross-country as well, heading for California. We bullshit about what it's like to be on the road, how awful it is to drive 16 hours a day, and how sick we are of camping. Nick plays the guitar, and I try to learn a few new chords from him. We watch their camp-

A black helicopter hovers overhead.

fire bloom and then die. Before we leave, Jared gives us the phone number of the place where they'll be staying in San Francisco. He wants us to contact him for a follow-up interview. I don't think we will.

In the morning, Jared and Nick pack up their gear and leave early. Matt and I do our laundry, hanging our shirts on a line stretched between two of the shelter's support posts. As we eat breakfast, we hear the sputtering belch of aircraft overhead. In the UFO pantheon, black heli-copters are the U.S. government's watchdogs, following flying saucers everywhere and terrorizing the people who witness the outerworldly craft. It is a little eerie for us then, to discover one buzzing above.

What is the helicopter doing here? Matt spots a red cross painted on it and speculates that the helicopter is participating in the military exercises taking place in Roswell this weekend. I prefer to imagine that the heli-copter has come because we've just encountered two beings from another planet: Nick and Jared. I hope we didn't tell them too much.

Crash

White Sands, New Mexico
June 6, 1996
J.F.

For the people who live near New Mexico's White Sands Missile Range, lights in the sky are an everyday occurrence. Stray missiles have facilitated UFO sightings in the surrounding area for years. According to Kevin D. Randle's *A History of UFO Crashes*, a flying saucer might have landed in Tularosa, N.Mex., inside White Sands Missile Range, in July, 1947 (amazingly, the same month and year as the Roswell incident). The evidence, however, is highly speculative, and Randle labels the event as having "insufficient data" to properly be determined genuine or a hoax. To the staid White Sands locals, it's a simple matter of logic: Flying saucers may be a hot topic, but here, we're grounded in reality. In spite of these dismissive explanations, or more likely, because of them, the

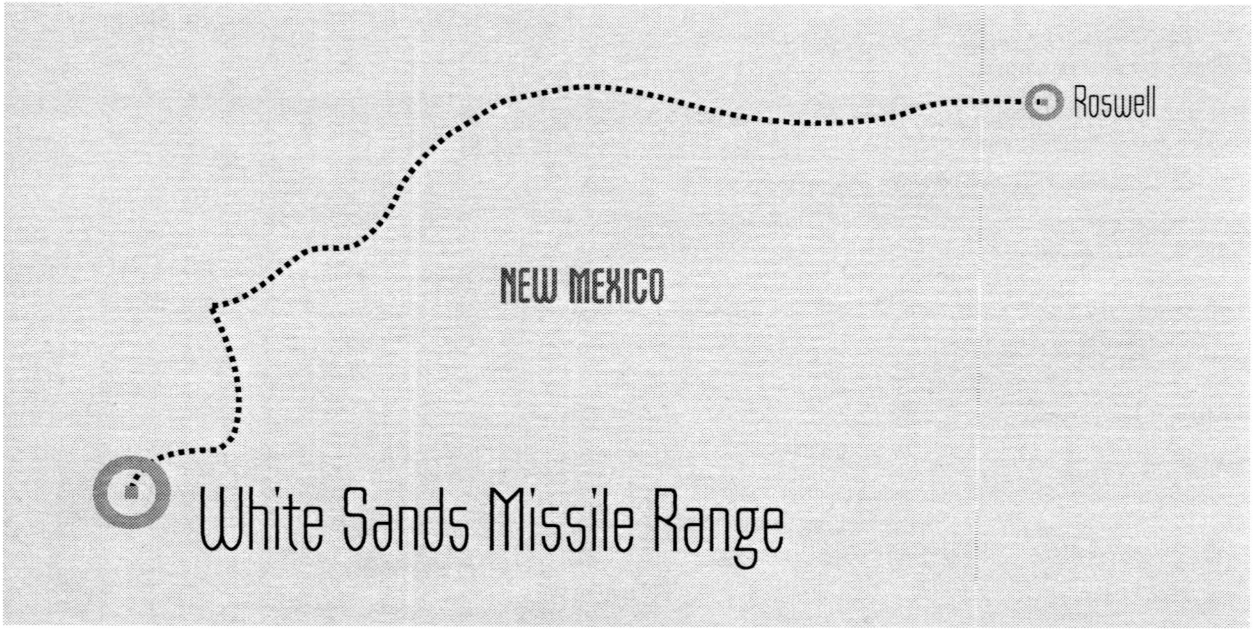

Roswell
NEW MEXICO
White Sands Missile Range

question has been raised time and again: What if just one of those lights isn't a missile? After all, Roswell, king of the UFO sites, is a mere hop, jump, and saucer skip across the New Mexican desert.

In the spirit of conspiracy, many modern UFO hunters have adopted the theory that Uncle Sam is hiding a few flying saucers up his red, white, and blue sleeves. Investigating U.S. military installations is a matter of UFOlogical practice that Matt and I are more than willing to follow. But, as we make our way to White Sands, we're unsure of what to expect. After all, we're not pros. This is the first time either of us will have visited a military installation with the intention of uncovering hidden information. Even if we don't take ourselves seriously, who's to say the MPs won't?

Driving down U.S. Route 70, it's not long before we see, by the side of the road, a huge sign flanked by what appear to be two faux missiles. The sign reads, in big, blocky letters: "UNITED STATES ARMY TEST AND EVALUATION COMMAND, WHITE SANDS MISSILE RANGE, NEW MEXICO." Printed near the words are two mysterious round insignias, perhaps denoting the military divisions stationed at the test site.

When we reach the range, we opt not to go to the Visitor's Center. They don't allow cameras, video, or audio taping on site, and our car is full of devices meant for that purpose. Sometimes security is just too much trouble. Instead, we make a beeline for a desolate part of the missile range border, Hi-8 ready to go.

The U.S. military does love its protocol. The chain link gate that blocks the road to the test site is covered with

An invitation to enter?

signs sporting a range of colors from bright caution yellow to pioneer brown. Rotting plywood backings which perhaps once supported sheets of metal with intimidating messages also decorate the entrance. The sign that attracts my attention says "NOTICE: MILITARY POLICE DO NOT LOCK THIS GATE, BY ORDER OF THE WSMR PROVOST MARSHAL." If the MPs have followed their orders, then anyone can push open the gate and drive his vehicle down the dirt road. However, several rusted chains and a padlock say differently. To the right is a cattle gate, a bridge-like contraption made up of metal slats positioned about two inches apart. The bridge is designed so people and cars can easily cross, but the hooves of the cattle slip between the slats, preventing them from proceeding. This particular entranceway is made impassable to cars by a wire stretched across its front and padlocked on one end.

However, other than the locked gates barring vehicles from entering, there are no security measures which would prevent the arrival of unwanted visitors. Any White Sands investigators who wish to trespass on government property could easily do so on foot. It seems the surrounding terrain is the true guardian of the test site. Because the land between us and the nearest buildings is so completely flat, and the sparse brush provides little, if any, cover, military personnel can easily see someone coming from far away.

Beyond the cattle gate wire, the dirt road wriggles its way through the dead, brown earth towards a set of run-down-looking structures. Telephone poles line the path that first leads to a small building with a slanted roof. Farther up the road is a squat warehouse. A dull pickup with a trailer carrying small, thin cylinders is parked out front, along with a number of other cars noticeably worn by the attrition of the sand.

The remaining stretch of road visible to us leads to a white, geodesic dome that sits patiently atop a box-shaped platform. Matt guesses that it's one of the radar monitoring stations for the missile range. A set of stairs

The WSMR dome

In the distance, the buildings of White Sands Missile Range

climbs to the platform.

To the left of these buildings, in the distance, I can see the bulk of the base, small white boxes nestled in the desert scrub, covered by the haze of the day's heat. There's no sign of any guards or any Grays, but given our propensity for putting ourselves in odd situations I'm not so sure we should enter. UFOs or no, I'm sure videotaping on U.S. military property isn't exactly condoned, and the few bucks that we've saved for this trip could in no way cover the medical expenses for stitching up bullet wounds. More realistically, we don't want to pay a fine or have our video camera taken away. We shoot some footage on our side of the fence, and I rant about the perils of government secrecy.

Stymied by the military, our only recourse is to talk to the locals. We climb back into the Geo and drive. Not far from White Sands, we happen upon the Star Wars Deli. This is very good, we think, and we stop to buy gas.

The entire front of the store is paneled like a suburban den. A sad-looking pleather couch that seems like it was recently divorced from a passenger van sits on a two-step concrete porch outside. Two of its brothers, resting in the shade nearby, offer their condolences. The Deli marquee reads "MAG-ZINES" and "7-11," which I assume is the store's hours of operation, not its corporate affiliation. A white placard in the window announces a "WARNING IN FORCE." This place, like the missile range, has too many signs.

Matt and I enter the deli, camera on. An old woman with faded golden hair sits behind the counter. Certainly she must have witnessed something mysterious, working so close to the range. I introduce myself and Matt and explain what we're up to. She tells me her name is Irene.

"Have you seen any strange lights in the sky or any other UFO-related phenomena?" I ask.

"No," Irene replies, staring at me from behind the cash register with a look one reserves for encyclopedia sales-men and door-to-door evangelists.

"What's the reason for naming your deli 'Star Wars,' then?" I ask.

"From the laser program President Nixon, I mean Reagan, wanted in. Shooting down planes," she replies.

"Not UFOs?"

George Lucas would be proud.

C'mon, Irene.

"No, no," she insists. It seems I'm getting nowhere here.

"How long has the Star Wars Deli been around?" I ask feebly.

"Ten years," she says.

"I bet George Lucas could sue this place out of business for copyright infringement," I think to myself. "There you have it, folks," I announce aloud to the camera. "Straight to you from the Star Wars Deli in White Sands, N.Mex."

As we drive away, leaving the Star Wars Deli behind, we pass one final sign, the size of a billboard. It reads, "WHEN FLASHING U.S. 70 CLOSED 13 MILES AHEAD. EXPECT ONE HOUR MAXIMUM DELAY." Apparently, the military doesn't want civilians cruising on the highway when they're testing rockets. On the sign to the left of the warning and above the words "WHITE SANDS MISSILE RANGE," there's a poor illustration of a military base with a rocket taking off from it. Smoke and orange flames are shooting out of the rocket's tail. The warning lights are dead, but it would matter little if they were blinking. White Sands has already defeated us.

Money for Nothing

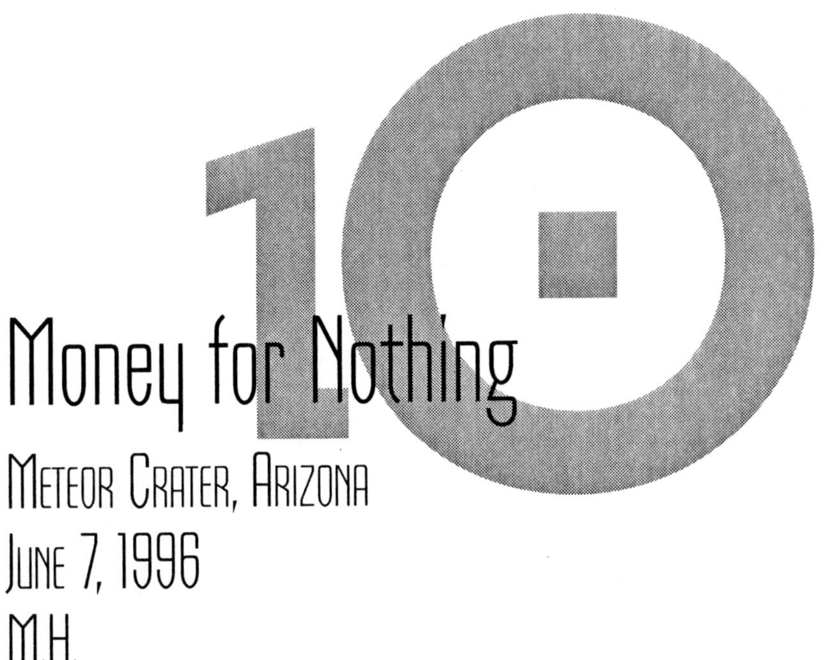

Meteor Crater, Arizona
June 7, 1996
M.H.

Arizona's desert climate dries, bakes, and cracks everything in sight, and the wind and water do clean-up, carv-
ing up the land and carrying it off grain by grain. This is
one beat-up state. The towers and gorges of the Painted
Desert, the Grand Canyon, and today's ultimate destination, Sedona, all attest to the rough history of this hot slab
of earth. But nowhere is the abuse more glaring than at
the Barringer Meteor Crater, just off Interstate 40, halfway
between Winslow and Flagstaff.

We feel some of it, baking under the Arizona sky as we
pull off the highway and onto the side road that leads
past a gas station and trailer park (also run by the crater
folks) toward Barringer Crater. We spent last night in
Holbrook, Ariz., because Snowflake, Ariz. had no hotels.

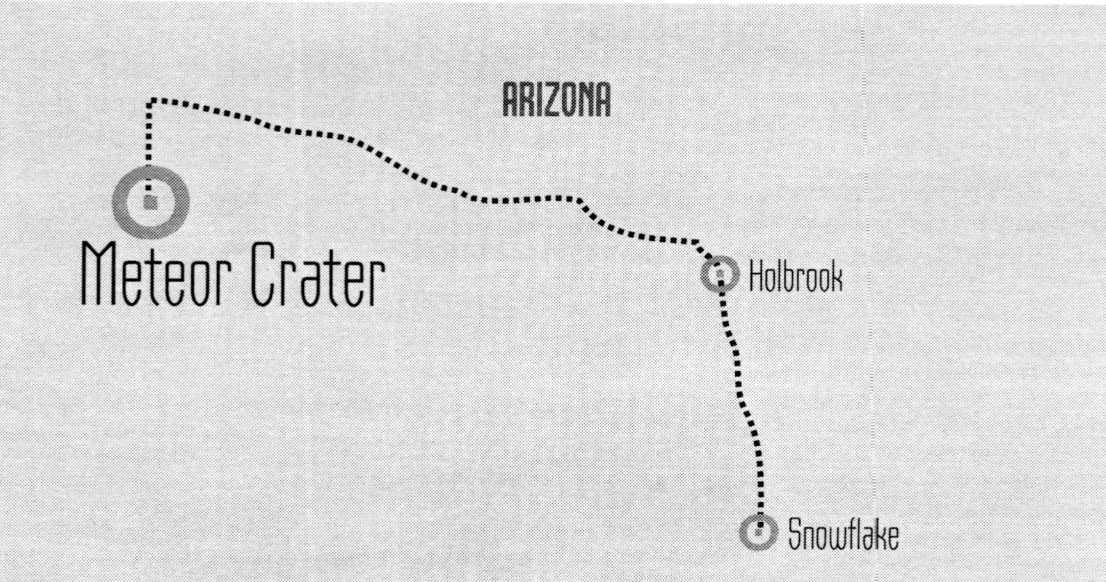

ARIZONA
Meteor Crater
Holbrook
Snowflake

Nor did it have Travis Walton, the abductee of *Fire in the Sky* fame. We had hoped to interview him and videotape the abduction site, but Walton is in Brazil.

After the disappointment of White Sands and Snowflake, our spirits are low. We go to Meteor Crater maybe for some inspiration: Here's a place where something from outer space has definitely touched the earth. Here is proof and science and a little dignity given to the investigation of extraterrestrial objects. I park the car in a crowded lot below the crater and climb into the noontime sun. Opening the car door is like opening the door to an oven.

What can you say about the Barringer Crater—or, as it is more popularly known, Meteor Crater—except the brutally obvious? It's a big hole in the ground. A *really* big hole in the ground. Fifty thousand years ago, a hunk of iron and nickel 150 feet in diameter hammered itself into the desert floor. The 20-megaton explosion killed all life within several miles of the impact site and tossed the topsoil, boulders, and bedrock like salad. Once everything had settled down, the really big hole was 550 feet deep and more than 4,000 feet across.

The natural human reaction to such an awesome natural wonder is, of course, to exploit it. At the turn of the century, Daniel Moreau Barringer saw the site as the perfect iron mine—the meteorite was presumably buried beneath the crater floor, waiting to be dug up and smelted down. He acquired rights to the crater in 1903 and spent 26 years trying to find the iron ore, but with no success. (Scientists have since hypothesized that the explosive impact vaporized the meteorite entirely.) In the for-

A whole lot of nothing

ties, people tried to extract the silica for glass manufacture, but gave up after hauling out only a few hundred tons. The sixties saw NASA using the crater as a training site, as it was remarkably similar to any that astronauts might encounter on the moon.

Today, the crater is still owned by the Barringer family, although Meteor Crater Enterprises, Inc. manages the RV park and gas station out near I-40 and the visitors' center perched on the rim of the crater. Here, a museum and gift shop, plus well-maintained vantage points on the crater rim, draw in 300,000 visitors every year. At $8 a head, it seems that Mr. Barringer (or his family, at least) has finally turned a profit, charging eager tourists for a gander at what is technically nothing—just a lack of dirt. It's all a testament to mankind's ability to wring a buck out of anything it puts its mind to, even a big empty hole in the ground.

At Graceland and Roswell, we expected commercialism. That was virtually the only reason to *go* to Roswell. But here, it's unexpected and unwelcome. I'm sure operating costs have to be met and all, but $16 for the both of us is a bit exorbitant for permission to look at a *hole*. And, of course, we're restricted to just the walkways at the one end, can't go into the crater, and so on.

We leave, beaten again, sucked dry by the hot sun and

Meteor Crater Enterprises, Inc. As we drive west into the endless desert, less than halfway through our trip with no hope in sight, unable to keep food chilled in our cooler for even a day, we know that something's going to break.

UFO Spirits

Sedona, Arizona/Mount Shasta, California
June 7, 1996
J.F.

Arizona is burning. It's only late spring, but even the shade cast by the canopy of evergreens overhead cannot dispel the dry heat that hangs expectantly in the air. There is an "extreme fire danger" warning for the entire state. As we set up our camp, the park caretaker informs us that we cannot have an open fire tonight or smoke cigarettes. We'll have to grab dinner in town.

Matt and I are approximately fifteen miles from Sedona, Ariz., a center of mysterious "earth energies" or "vortices" that has attracted members of the New Age community in droves. One scientific explanation for these alleged forces is electromagnetism caused by a high concentration of iron oxide in the rock formations around Sedona. New Agers prefer a more mystical explanation: To the ini-

Flagstaff
Meteor Crater
Sedona
ARIZONA
OREGON
PACIFIC OCEAN
Mt. Shasta
CALIFORNIA

tiated, a vortex is a spiritual well that has the ability to enhance psychic talents such as clairvoyance and channeling by putting Man in direct contact with Mother Earth. Matt and I are in Sedona because, according to UFO lore, alien beings have a profound interest in vortex energy and appear in the area as frequently as the New Agers. Sightings abound here. Channeling—receiving information from beings on other planes of existence through a form of meditation—is also big in Sedona. Sometimes, channelers claim, the beings they communicate with are extraterrestrials.

Matt and I finish putting up the tent, climb in the car, and venture into Sedona. We park the Geo in town, and Matt hunts for information while I take a nap in the vehicle. He returns from his mission sooner than I'd hoped he would. I groggily sit up and rub my eyes.

"What do you think we should do first?" Matt asks as he sits back down in the driver's seat of the Geo. I'm hungry, burnt out, and finding it impossible to think clearly. Matt shuffles through a handful of brochures and leaflets he has collected.

"We could check out one of these New Age psychics or take a look at the shops," Matt offers. We have a lot of ground to cover here in Sedona, but I can't seem to concentrate on the task at hand.

"Look at this," Matt says, pointing to a flyer. "We can have our auras read or discover our past lives through hypnotic regression."

Sedona is too much for me. Instead of answering Matt's question, I laugh. "Hey. What's wrong with you?" he demands.

"I don't know. I'm feeling light-headed," I say. "This trip's beginning to wear on me."

I attempt to remove the cobwebs from my mind as we saunter along the main drag with the other tourists. The crowd circulating through Sedona's dusty streets is predominantly forty-something and quasi-spiritual, judging from the crystals on their necklaces and bracelets. The shops lining the road reflect the tourist audience's taste in wares: New Age merchandise, Indian crafts, and leather goods. We walk past a disheveled man who's leaning on a wooden fence, muttering to himself. I can't understand what he's saying, but I'm sure he feels as fried as I do. We finally stop at a store that sells jewelry and books on topics such as paganism, witchcraft, and meditation. I want to find a reference that puts New Age beliefs, UFOs, and Sedona into perspective.

The New Age movement is a search for the sacred, but the rules are not set in stone. New Agers encourage spiritual freedom, and because of this, the threads that connect the whole movement are loosely knit. New Age beliefs can be difficult to define. Ideology draws upon a variety of traditions including Christianity, Buddhism, Hinduism, and Shamanism. Meditation is a method for spiritual growth and crystals hold immeasurable power. Psychic abilities, like channeling and clairvoyance, are underdeveloped human talents. For some New Agers, UFOs and aliens are facts of life, and the reemergence of ancient civilizations such as Atlantis, glimpses of the future. In the New Age community, judging others' beliefs is a definite faux pas. However, there seems to be little acceptance of "negative energy." Followers of the New Age encourage love, respect for nature, and positive spirituality.

At the store, I purchase a silver ring and two books, *The Mysteries of Sedona* and *The Alien Tide,* both by local author Tom Dongo. According to Dongo, people from all over the country are inexplicably and irresistibly drawn to Sedona. In *The Mysteries of Sedona,* he describes the "typical story" of a New Age pilgrim:

> "I felt such a strong pull to Sedona that after a period of time, Sedona became an obsession. One day the decision was made; I quit my secure job, sold my house, said good-bye to my astonished friends and relatives, and moved two thousand miles to a place I had never seen … When I arrived, I felt I had come home!"

The reason for this urge is unclear, but apparently the aliens feel it as well. Matt and I want to tap into the energy.

Dongo states in *The Mysteries of Sedona* that "There are four primary/stationary focuses of Sedona's vibrant energies at this time. They are Bell Rock, Cathedral Rock, Boynton Canyon and the Airport Vortex." We decide to investigate the Airport Vortex because it's located on a mesa relatively close to town. We pick up a free map of Sedona and head off in what we hope is the right direction. Unfortunately, we soon discover that "free" is really another way of saying, "so cheap we couldn't be bothered to mark the location of the vortices with any degree of accuracy." We understand that the art of finding vortices is

View from the Airport Vortex

not an exact science, but we quickly become frustrated when we realize there are no markers, no signs, no hovering spacecraft, nothin' except spiritual direction which, at the moment, we seem to be lacking. But we're on the road, and it's too late to turn back now. We drive out to a spot near the airport and decide that we're close enough. After all, we're amateurs. We get out of the car, attempt to feel the energy of this "Masculine and Creative Vortex," and are greeted with a degree of success. We film a mildly amusing bit for our Hi-8 documentary. The earth energy has, no doubt, inspired us. Neither Matt nor I are quite sure what to make of the vortex phenomenon yet.

We decide to eat at a diner back on Sedona's main road. Not five minutes after we're seated at a booth, the topic of God's existence comes up. Matt's spiritual beliefs fall squarely into the atheist/agnostic camp, while I am a born-and-bred Baptist. We have debated this subject many times, neither able to convince the other of his perspective. So, it isn't surprising that when the waitress arrives to take our order, we are deep in the theological trenches. We select our food quickly so we can return to our debate as soon as possible. The argument heats up and by the end of the conversation it's evident that the other customers in the restaurant are either eavesdropping on us or trying to ignore the ignorant loudmouths from back East, as the case may be. There is no doubt in my mind that Sedona's emphasis on the spiritual has something to do with our discussion, but as to whether this is energy coming from the vortex or just our surroundings in general is impossible to tell. Matt and I are both looking for further spiritual understanding, and, on this trip, we have learned not to ignore coincidence. Coincidence is the key to the realm of God, miracles, and maybe even UFOs. We both agree that regardless of whether you define the energy as magnetic or spiritual, there is a powerful force present in Sedona. It, at least for a little while, has made our lives stranger than usual. No wonder the aliens like it here. We pay the bill and head back to the camp.

Nearly two weeks pass before coincidence strikes again. We're driving through California, when we make a random pit stop at a gas station to call Paul Trent, who snapped the first UFO photos in 1950. Trent's photos have never been proven hoaxes, and we're itching to interview him. The woman at the counter asks about my UFO T-shirt, and when I explain the nature of our trip, she suggests that we interview some of the local residents. Apparently, sightings are common in this neck of the woods. Where are we? Mt. Shasta, Calif., another earth vortex and apparent attraction point for extraterrestrial activity. Matt and I decide to take a look around town.

But first, the phone call. Mrs. Trent answers. When I

inform her of our desire to talk to her husband, she explains that Paul Trent is not in good health and does not like to do interviews. She further stipulates that if we wish to speak with Paul, we'll have to pay herself and her husband $100 each, an impossibility given the amount of money we have left. I can only suppose that mad-dog journalists have taken their toll on this couple in the 46 years since Trent took the UFO photos. I politely decline her offer, hang up the phone, and go back to the car.

We stop at a New Age bookstore across the street from the gas station, where I pick up a copy of the local magazine *Directions*. According to its subhead, *Directions* provides "Transformational Information from the Vortex of Mount Shasta." The advertisements that litter this publication provide further insight into the New Age movement. On the back page, super blue-green algae is touted as a health supplement. The ad claims that "commonly reported results" from the use of the algae include "reduction of the symptoms of fatigue, hypoglycemia, PMS, stress/depression/anxiety, and allergies." All-natural health foods and a vegetarian diet are integral parts of the New Age lexicon. Here, in another ad, is the belief in the power of crystals and the like. "Treat yourself to beautiful jewelry that helps align and balance your energy field," a full-pager hawking "light energy" pendants encourages. Keth Luke, "Master of Light," offers "Soulbody Work," a "divine tune up for you and your group." Luke promises he will "shift your soul, flush out your past, grease the gears of growth, attune and upgrade your vehicle" through such services as "brain repatterning, soul retrieval, Karmic clearing, self-healing of dis-ease and mental illness, and soul, DNA and healer attunement." Keth also offers to "remove or install probes and implants." Why would you want to install an implant? This guy has got to be in league with the Grays. According to the ad, Luke's credentials include "etheric surgeon, 8th degree Reiki master, minister, shaman, exorcist, and astrologer."

I peruse the editorial text, which is made up mostly of columns by Hindu monks, spiritual teachers, and New Age authors with eclectic claims to fame like "founder of the Golden Dolphin Project, a school for evolutionary healing and training." Among other topics, the columns discuss meditation, love, karma, and respect for the environment.

The ads in *Directions* only emphasize what the rest of the world finds so unbelievable and maybe even laughable about the New Age movement. While the benefits of blue-green algae may have some scientific merit, and "light-energy" pendants may bring their wearer a positive mind-set, removing and installing implants seems, at best, bizarre and silly. However, within the body text of the magazine are teachings and ideals, like environmentalism, that could very well benefit humanity. The problem for the New Age movement, then, is that these teachings are buried in muck that seems ridiculous to the modern world, and without the proper presentation, no one will listen. Drawing upon my Baptist upbringing, I ponder the fact that many Biblical prophets were similarly ignored and laughed at. Perhaps the nature of the teachings, not their presentation, is what's truly important.

The connection between New Ageism and extraterres-

Intergalactic Delights

trials is hazy. In general, extraterrestrials are seen as beings that dwell on a higher evolutionary plane and humanity is seen as an infant race that must work immeasurably hard to get there. The further evolution of man is New Ageism's ultimate goal. In *The Mysteries of Sedona*'s concluding chapter, Tom Dongo urges humanity to pay close attention to "the absolutely incredible recent rise in the frequency of alien being and space ship interactions with humanity worldwide." Dongo goes on to say that "we need to recognize the reality that these entities exist and establish some kind of working, beneficial relationship with these beings, or at least one race, as soon as safely possible. The ignorance is on our side, not theirs."

I glance around the bookstore and see that the locals have made themselves scarce. Believing that we'll find nothing of further interest in Mt. Shasta, Matt and I start upon our journey back to the highway. Almost immediately, we spot Intergalactic Delights, an ice-cream parlor and restaurant on the main road. Whoever or whatever is orchestrating these coincidences apparently also has a sense of humor. Every good UFOlogist knows that the captive Gray aliens in Nevada's underground bases love ice cream—especially strawberry. We pull over.

Inside Intergalactic Delights, I ask the girl at the counter whether or not she has seen any lights in the sky or extraterrestrial activity in the area. She's startled by my questions and looks too embarrassed to answer. The fact that Matt is recording the interview with the Hi-8 camera probably isn't helping. I finally convince her to tell me why she lives in Mt. Shasta, and she explains that she was attracted to the spiritual aspects of the mountain. However, she has never seen any UFOs. I ask her, then, why she's working at Intergalactic Delights. She shrugs. The money's just too good to pass up, I suppose.

As Matt and I are leaving the restaurant, an older woman, apparently also an Intergalactic Delights employee, follows us outside and tells us that she has spotted UFOs near Mt. Shasta. Her name is Donna, and she appears to be in her mid-30s. Donna has frizzy brown hair, a motherly, careworn face, and is wearing a baby-blue sweater with a host of fuzzy nobs on it. She seems rational, honest, and eager to talk with us. We interview her on the tree-lined sidewalk in front of a sign that says, "Cafe." Cars drift along the street, and pedestrians make their way by us, sleepily trudging through the warm summer day.

"I used to live about three miles up the mountain," Donna begins. "And, I've seen various UFOs in the 18 years I've been here."

"Have these been just lights in the sky or have you actually seen a landing?" I ask.

"I haven't seen a landing," she replies. "A couple of times

Donna waves.

I have seen lights in the sky—definitely UFOs. One time, when I was driving towards the mountain, I looked up, and saw about a dozen silver ships. The minute I noticed them, I turned my head. Then I remembered that I saw them, and I looked back, but they were gone. That's happened several times when I've seen UFOs—where I've actually gone towards them, and they've disappeared, like they somehow know. I'm not a UFO enthusiast, but I have seen them here."

The spiritual side of UFO activity and abductions is an odd one to say the least. Harvard psychiatrist and author Dr. John Mack has suggested that alien abduction may very well occur in a realm that we can only describe, at present, as the spiritual. If this is true, then the vortices in Sedona and Mt. Shasta could indeed, as the New Agers claim, be direct mystical links to extraterrestrial beings on higher planes. But, for now, all this is speculation. The only thing I suppose we can do is pull up a lawn chair in front of Intergalactic Delights and wait. If they are coming, I'm sure they're going to want their strawberry ice cream.

Integratron

Landers, California
June 10, 1996
M.H.

12

s Juan Ponce de León learned when he traveled into the unknown wilds of the New World, eternal life can be elusive. Jon and I have been driving west across the Sonoran Desert for days, en route to George Van Tassel's legendary life-rejuvenating machine, the Integratron. Its whereabouts are poorly documented. Twentynine Palms. Joshua Tree. Giant Rock. All vague landmarks by the roadside, perhaps the inspiration to some heat-crazed adventurer of days long past who scribbled down their mythic names to guide him back yet confound others.

This morning we left Needles, Calif., forsaking the relative coolness beside the polluted Colorado River for the 122° F, shadeless, open desert in search of Twentynine Palms, Calif. Ill-marked roads, free of all traffic, led us fur-

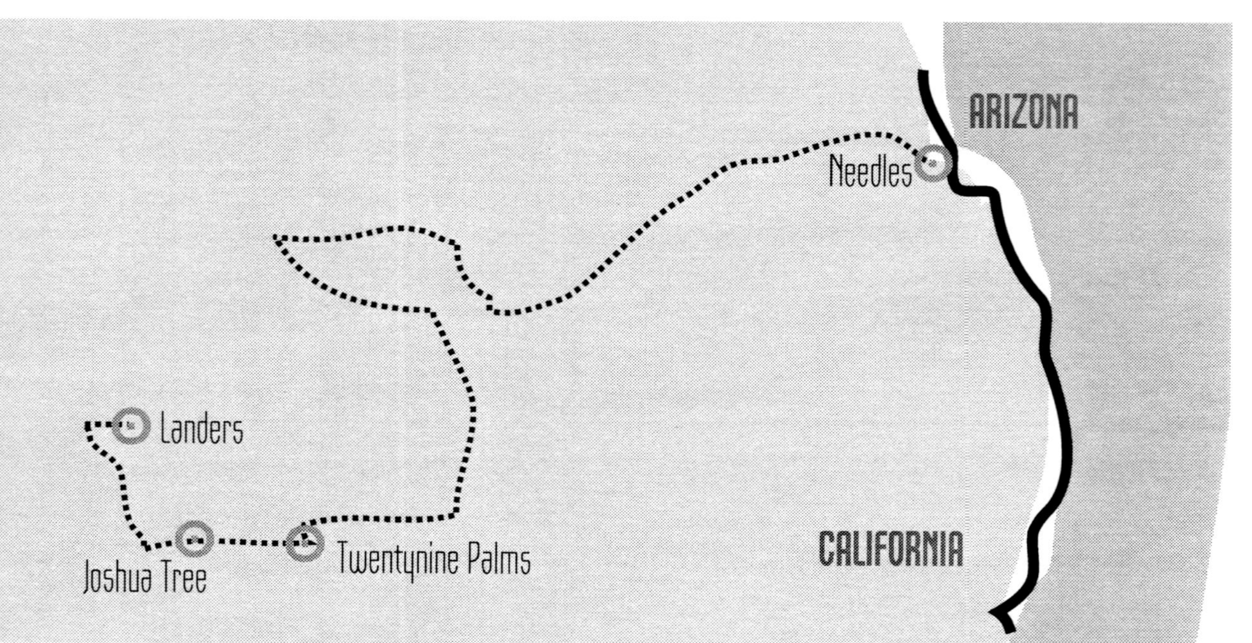

ARIZONA
CALIFORNIA
Needles
Landers
Joshua Tree
Twentynine Palms

ther and further from civilization and emergency aid, sending us on an unexpected 50-mile detour around road construction at the only town we encountered as our fuel gauge began to droop uncomfortably low. The town of Twentynine Palms finally appeared, an oasis blessed with life-giving gasoline and soda, but it was not the Cibola we had expected: No Integratron was to be found.

Thinking about it now, I don't know how we expected to find it—maybe 29 palm trees would line either side of a path leading directly to the Integratron's door like some mystical runway. I'm not even quite sure what an Integratron looks like—just that it has a dome on top and houses some sort of electrostatic generator meant to recharge cells in the body like batteries, resulting in extended youth and life. At the Twentynine Palms municipal building, the two employees on duty could find no record of it in their directories or maps, and calls they made to nearby townships yielded the same results. We left, dispirited, and are now trying to find our way to the next mysterious location associated with Van Tassel's Integratron—Joshua Tree.

Did you know that the cover of U2's album *The Joshua Tree* was photographed in Joshua Tree National Monument? Well, I didn't—just never gave it much thought, or put two and two together. Standing there in the park, you can see that it's the same place as on the album, and realize that the photograph conveys absolutely nothing of the experience of Joshua Tree. Well, maybe a little. I now understand why the guys in the band look so annoyed— they had to wear those heavy wool coats in the middle of a burning desert. Bono's probably ready to pass out.

Joshua Tree is like the friggin' moon—all barren rock and sand, bizarre terrain, no animal life in sight. The meager flora looks like a dried flower arrangement, brown and papery. But even though alien beings directed Van Tassel to build the Integratron, its otherworldly silhouette is noticeably absent in the moonlike park and in the adjacent town of Joshua Tree. We drive our little purple lunar rover back to the front entrance of the park and I go into the gift shop to appeal for help.

"Can you tell me where Giant Rock is?" I ask a woman behind the information desk, playing my last card, our resources exhausted so early in the day. The woman, late forties with drab blond curls, narrows her eyes and suspiciously asks why I want to go *there*. The parental tone tells me right away that Giant Rock is a place of ill repute. It's probably a teenage pot-smoking, beer-drinking hangout today. Probably was back in Van Tassel's day, too.

In 1947, he quit his job as a test pilot and aircraft engineer and leased the land that includes the current site of the Integratron and Giant Rock—believed to be the world's largest freestanding boulder—from the government. Van Tassel thought that the massive weight of Giant Rock produced a piezoelectric effect (applying pressure to piezoelectric crystals generates a small amount of electricity—for example, this is how electronic drum pads create signals when hit with drumsticks) on the boulder's granite crystals, generating an electromagnetic vortex. He and his family lived by the boulder, sleeping under the stars and using several small rooms that had been hollowed out beneath it (by the previous tenant, Frank

Critzer, who was killed when dynamite he had stored in the chambers exploded) for storage. They embraced meditation, universal love, and all that, and founded the College of Universal Wisdom to share the knowledge gleaned from psychic contact with aliens from Venus.

Jon and I are not here to drop acid and commune with Energy, though, so the woman's reaction takes me by surprise. I expect disbelief, people thinking we're crazy, or just hating us because we're drifters or from the East, but I don't know quite what to do with disapproval. Sure, maybe we're wasting our time, but the time's ours to waste. It's not like we're up to no good.

I decide to clarify, blurting "Integraton," and waving my hands and shaking my head to indicate that I'm not some pot-smoking, Phish-phollowing high schooler. "The Integraton. IntegraTRON?" Not only is it hard to find, but our sources couldn't agree on the spelling of the thing's name. Quickly, I explain that we're looking for the Integratron and had been told that it was near Giant Rock—which isn't listed on our maps.

"Oh," she says. "It's not near *there.*" Pulling out a piece of paper and a pen, the woman dictates directions to me in a shaking-her-head, tsk-tsking kind of way, only now it's because I'm a doofus rather than a delinquent.

So as we leave yet another town, moving on to our absolute last clue, we find a new name to put into the annals of the Integratron legend: the town of Landers. Town is too strong a word, for Landers is just a bunch of roads through the arid, low-hilled land, interrupted by the occasional house, trailer, or farm. As per the directions, we

The jungle gym

turn off of Old Woman Springs Road at the sign for Gubbler's Orchids and, a few minutes later, blow right past the white-domed Integratron and have to turn around.

On a dirt road next to the property, we park. Trailer homes stand within view of us, but no one comes to complain when we get out to inspect the scene, cameras in hand. The Integratron's fenced in—thrice—but the outer ring of chain link has fallen open and curls along the ground, allowing us enough room to drive the car through, if we wished. The second perimeter sports a barbed-wire haircut, but some fool has left the gate unlocked. We go by foot, trespassing lightly on the grounds of the seemingly unoccupied Integratron.

A few odd, but very decrepit, features mark the dusty, scrubby ground. Nearest to the main road, a rusty, saucer-shaped jungle gym lies, toppled, on a small rise. Closer to our car sits a tweaked-out Volkswagen Beetle, its engine cover plate (I guess you could call it the hood, except that it's in the back) removed to expose the bulging machinery and tubes like some neurosurgery patient lying on a table, the top of his cranium temporarily missing. An above-ground swimming pool calls to us invitingly through the desert heat with whirring filters, but as Jon hoists his head above the six-foot-high rim, he declares that the water is full of green algae. Perhaps the filters are actually some sort of life-support machinery for the foreign sludge.

Centrally situated on the property is the white dome of the Integratron—38 feet high, 50 feet across, and non-metallic to prevent interference with magnetic fields—like a slightly flat observatory cut through with tiny, dark windows. Chain link topped with barbed wire decorated with a "VOLTAGE" badge encloses the electrostatic wonder. The left half of the "VOLTAGE" sign seems to have fallen off, likely taken by some young punk who wanted a "HIGH" sign for his room. Sure, the electric fence threat is probably just a ruse, but neither of us wants to test it out. Jon and I are the best kind of trespassers to have on your property. We obey all signs that promise bodily injury.

I also consider that the "(HIGH) VOLTAGE" warning may

Breaking and entering? That's for the courts to decide.

Voltage

refer to the Integratron itself, rather than the fence—a good warning, indeed, since the structure itself might be dangerous. Van Tassel had some strange notions about physics and biology: In a paper on the workings of the Integratron, he noted that "Cilia in the lungs and respiratory tract are antennae that extract radiations from the air and transmit this energy to the cells in the blood to be conveyed throughout the body." Most of the world thinks that the lungs extract *oxygen* from the air, rather than radiations, but George's independent spirit was unquenchable. He held UFO conferences at Giant Rock to raise money for the construction of the Integratron, and worked on it until the end of his life in 1978. Afterwards it fell into disrepair and went through the hands of a number of owners. At one point, it was a disco.

A cop car prowls by and then goes away while Jon is busy tossing rocks at the electric fence, but I don't bring it to his attention. He's prone to paranoid episodes and the rest of our brief visit would be shot if he started worrying about cops. Out by the roadside I find a sign that has fallen to the ground, declaring open house hours for the

Integratron. (Finally, the proper spelling.) A group headed by San Francisco radio producer Emile Canning bought the structure in 1987, and now holds open houses and rents it out for New Age spiritual events and seminars. Canning is still exploring ways to bring the Integratron into full operation.

And that's the kicker. Like some Greek tragedy, George Van Tassel's tale ends with crushing irony. Forget sleeping with your own mother, killing your father, or even wishing for eternal life without specifying eternal youth, and remember that the Integratron was only 82% complete when work ceased in 1978. Here Van Tassel had a machine that would grant eternal life, *but he died before he could finish it.* We pull out of the dusty drive and start making our way to our next destination, Mt. Palomar, glad to know that even George Van Tassel had a hard time finding the fountain of youth.

Integratron. I-N-T-E-G-R-A-T-R-O-N. Integratron.

Ambassador to the Stars

Mount Palomar, California
June 10, 1996
M.H.

t. Palomar is not rip-roaring excitement. It's not very awe-inspiring as mountains go: A gentle (if extraordinarily long) road climbs the mountain, surrounded by ordinary trees and even the occasional house to render the overall impression of a steep, sparsely populated suburb. As the road goes on and on, we realize that the only real danger is the lack of gas stations.

Were you an astronomer, it might be different. One can't help but admit that the Mt. Palomar Observatory has turned out some interesting stuff, and that it must be wild to look at the universe through a 200-inch telescope, even if most of the work that goes along with it—photographing, cataloguing, marking exact azimuth and time and whatnot—is pretty grueling. Sure, we've spent a lot of

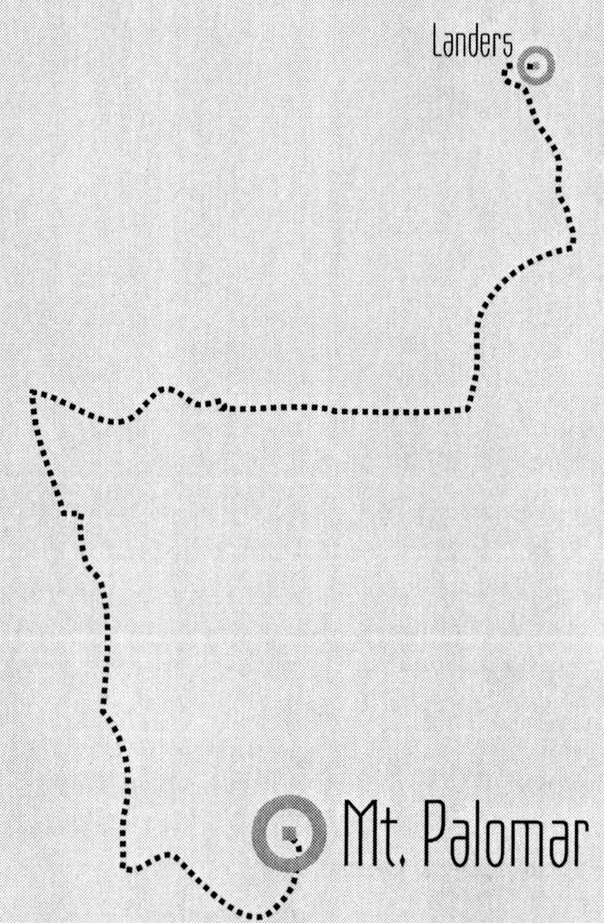

CALIFORNIA
Landers
Mt. Palomar

time looking at the night sky on our trip, but driving around the country searching for UFOs still doesn't exactly make us astronomers. As a result, when we arrive a bit too late for visiting hours, we can't even get in to see the domes. All this travel, and it's closed. We look at the bar that half-crosses the driveway, hindering us only symbolically. Even the Integratron was shut tighter, but unfortunately, we figure that people actually care about Palomar—making it a hundred times more likely that we'd get busted—and trespassers might have to duke it out with frustrated Astronomy Ph.D. candidates. After some filming, we coast back down the mountain. Literally: We're almost out of gas, so I throw the car into neutral and stay away from the pedals as much as possible.

Mt. Palomar holds the distinction of being the site of the first human contact with extraterrestrial intelligence. It occurred not in the observatory, as one might think, but in a hamburger stand just down the mountain. At least, that's where the ambassador worked. In 1953, George Adamski, a short-order cook who worked near Palomar, released the book *Flying Saucers Have Landed,* in which he claimed that he had had telepathic contact with alien beings from Venus while driving through the California desert. This was in the days before we learned that Venus is a high-pressure, sulfuric-acid hell, so he brought the world wildly inaccurate descriptions of the aliens' watery home.

Adamski turned the UFO field into something of the media frenzy it is today, touring on the lecture circuit, giving radio interviews, and setting the format for all UFO contactee/researcher personalities that were to follow,

On top of Mt. Palomar, moments too late

right up to the present day. He also pushed the standard "Space Brothers" line—as did George Van Tassel—where the aliens in the rest of the universe are all united in peace and love and very alarmed that we have nukes.

And George flipped burgers. We finally make contact of a sort, finding a country store and restaurant halfway down the mountain—close enough, at least for this pilgrimage, to Adamski's cafe. The building doesn't look more than ten years old, but sitting on the porch are two men in their sixties or seventies who look like they've been on the mountain since 1953. And maybe they have. When we ask if any other restaurants are nearby (no) and then explain why we're on Mt. Palomar in the first place, they tell us that they remember old George Adamski. "People 'round here used to call him 'Ol' Damn Nasty,'" one chuckles. Not a very grand reception for Earth's first interplanetary ambassador.

We climb back in the car and sail on down the mountain again. Night is falling: time for us to head for El Cajon, where our next meeting awaits us in the morning; time for interplanetary dignitaries and grad students to divine meaning from the stars.

From the Insane Planet of the Robots

El Cajon, California
June 11, 1996
M.H.

The new millennium is coming, but most people don't know when. Don't party like it's 1999, because the year 2000 means nothing. There never was a year Zero, so the year 2000 is still a part of the twentieth century, not the twenty-first, and we're all going to be jazzed about the wrong New Year's party. But don't worry—when the misplaced revelries die down and everyone thinks that they've got the hang of the twenty-first century (though it hasn't even arrived), we'll get a reminder.

In El Cajon, a city 16 miles east of San Diego, they know what time it is. They know that the new millennium starts in the year 2001, not the year 2000. It's the end of the Piscean Age and the dawning of the Age of Aquarius. And the New Age begins when Muons from the planet Myton

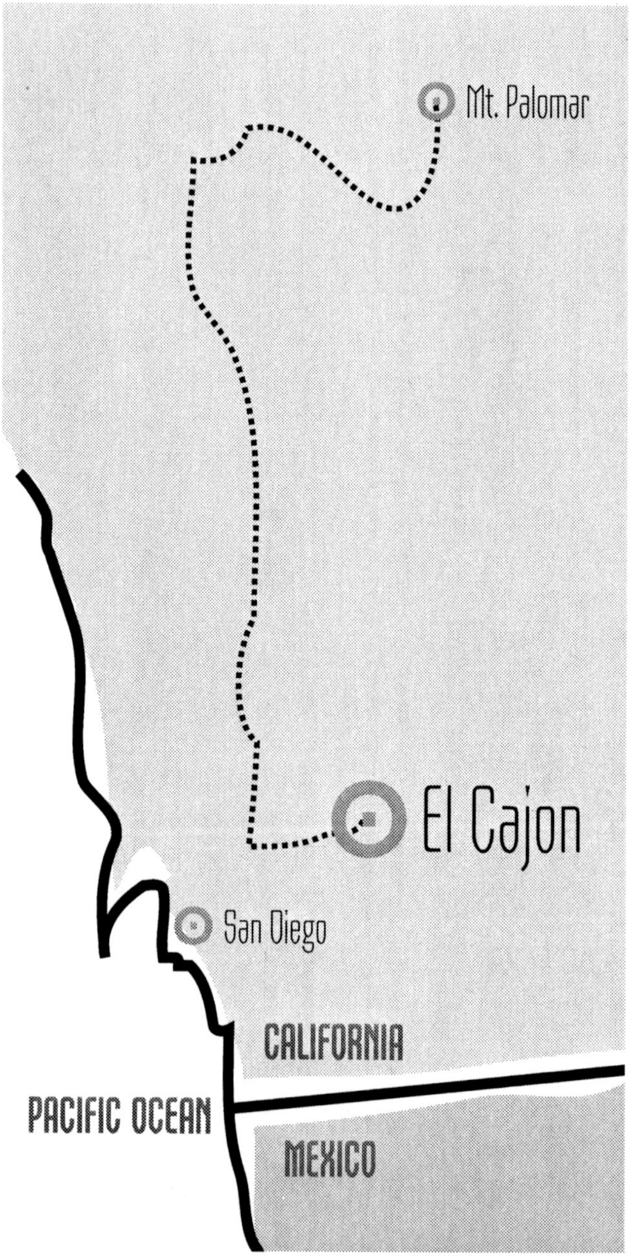

Mt. Palomar
El Cajon
San Diego
CALIFORNIA
PACIFIC OCEAN
MEXICO

complete their long journey from the Pleiades and land their spaceship on a portion of the lost continent of Atlantis that will rise from the Caribbean Sea, welcoming our planet as the 33rd member of the Interplanetary Confederation.

At the Unarius Academy of Science in El Cajon, the advance knowledge of the Muons and many higher spiritual beings has been received through astral channels and laid down in an ever-expanding library. But Unarius, founded in 1954 by Ruth Norman and her husband Ernest, is not mere New-Age huckstery. Unarius doesn't fall into any categories easily, and is both more and less than a UFO research group, a New Age college, a messianic cult, and a fashion nightmare on its way. But whatever your question, Unarius has an answer.

Jon and I, in our motel room in El Cajon, worry that we'll have a hard time finding Unarius. I tear their address from the phone book and we set out to find South Magnolia Avenue, hoping that it intersects Main Street, where our motel is located. El Cajon is an urban version of the isolated strip towns we've run across throughout the Southwest. The buildings and businesses—Jack-in-the-Boxes, gas stations, and cheap motels—share the same weathered desert decor but stand packed tightly together instead of being separated by dusty, scrub-grassed vacant lots. Barely two blocks from our motel, we spot the building.

On the side of a whitewashed wall, a 10-foot by 20-foot New Age mural of a starship coming to rest before a crystalline city on the edge of a purple sea sings out the presence of Unarius's home, the New World Teaching Center.

Are YOU ready for the arrival of flying saucers?

The mural borders a parking lot, so we pull in and park. Deep display windows that line the front of the building, flanking the door, suggest that the Center was once a store. In a rocky, dusty vacant lot across the street, Jon and I videotape a quick intro, the Center's façade with two-foot-tall red and blue letters spelling out "UNARIUS ACADEMY OF SCIENCE," "CENTER FOR THE NEW WORLD TEACHING," and "BOOKS TAPES LECTURES" in the background for easy identification.

An electronic door chime goes off as we enter the building, alerting the Unariuns to our presence. Cool air, soft light, and gentle music drift past a row of classical columns, crawling with tendrils of plastic ivy, that separate the large, open room. To the right lie sculptural artworks and models of the coming spacecraft and cities of the future, and to the left are a reading table and the massive library. Along the edge of a soffit above our heads, someone has painted the full text for which UNARIUS is an acronym: UNiversal ARticulate Interdimensional Understanding of Science. And, strangest of all, interspersed between bookshelves and pedestals around the room are portraits of the late Ernest and Ruth Norman, keeping watch over their vision of the future.

It's difficult to say whether the portraits of Ruth and Ernest are doctored photographs or trompe l'oeil paintings, but they are fairly honest. Ernest appears as an old, thin, slightly stooped man, but one that is nonetheless trying to smile cheerfully. Ruth, too, is old, though she seems terribly vibrant and alive compared to her somewhat tired-looking husband (who Ruth in fact outlived). And from corroborating photographs I've seen in Unarius's literature, it's clear that the artists took no liberties with Ruth's style of dress: metallic robe, cascading jewelry, tiara atop her golden curls, and magic wand in her hand. The portraitist may have embellished slightly when it came to the glowing halos surrounding her and Ernest, but then again, maybe such things don't show up on film, and the other photographs were wrong.

These "cosmic visionaries" (according to Unarius literature) channeled dozens of books during their most recent lifetimes. This information came from their higher selves: Ruth and Ernest are the archangels Uriel and Raphiel, respectively. Their higher selves, who know much more than can be squeezed into a mere earthbound brain, supplied information to Ruth and Ernest on the nature of physics, life and death, karma, and even the distant past and near future, forming the core of Unarius's teaching.

For some unknowable, divine reason, the Normans chose El Cajon as the place to establish their teaching sanctuary and stage their global (and interdimensional) operations. Unarius claims more than 500,000 students worldwide, and has Teaching Centers in El Cajon, New

York, Florida, North Carolina, Toronto, Paris, London, Turin, Madrid, Nigeria, and New Zealand, though only 75 students (none of whom appear to be in) are enrolled in classes at the home base, the El Cajon Center.

Just before we start to worry that no one is home, from a hallway towards the rear of the main room comes Carol Robinson, an older woman who says she used to work as a counseling psychologist. A student of the Unarius philosophy, Carol volunteers her time at the Center. She happily shows us around, explaining sculptures and paintings, letting me film at will. And, glad to inform us of Unarius's mission, she hands us a copy of the book *Preparation for the Landing: The Arrival* to supplement the more general literature we already possess, then goes off to find another student so that we can interview the two of them together.

I heft the heavy, hardcover book in my hand, and look to Jon. The dust jacket lists a price of $30.00. After the Leah Haley/Marc Davenport fiasco less than two weeks ago, we're both astonished that Unarius is letting us have this for free. I page through it while we wait for Carol's return, pondering the motives of Unarius and the nature of channeling, which produced this tome.

Channeling, I quickly conclude, is amazing—wisdom travels from the astral plane to the receiver to the typewriter without so much as a first edit. The book *Preparation for the Landing: The Arrival* is a terribly dense piece of literature chronicling those fateful days in 2001 when the Muons will finally land. Gripping passages like:

"The craft began its descent in an almost imperceptible movement. The ratio of the directional force in which this large spaceship was designed changed in its movement through outer space within the momentum, inertia, and gravity of the physical universe. Crossing through the meridian lines of the forces of the electromagnetic flux fields ..."

are laid down in Courier font for nearly 500 pages, fresh from the Smith-Corona to the bookbinder. Other fruits of channeling include Unarius's unique pastel-paletted artworks, like the mural on the wall outside, or one of the many depictions of the pastel-robed citizens of Atlantis, where traditional laws of drawing and perspective are laid aside for the sake of content in some strange, degenerate form of the Bob Ross tradition of painting. Or perhaps he, too, is now channeling painting lessons from the astral worlds. When we asked Carol about the various artworks during our brief tour, she remarked with wonder on the fact that, before the painters of the pictures came to Unarius, they "never even knew they were artists!" The loss to the world would be terrible, indeed, had such revelations not been made.

In a few minutes, Carol returns with Frank Sarlock, a hefty, jolly fellow with glasses, a bald head, and wisps of white hair. A salmon-colored, short-sleeved shirt is open to the middle of his chest. Frank, semiretired, volunteers his time here every day; he also has a business selling acoustic instruments, but says, "I try to spend more time here."

We agree that the reading table would be the best place to tape the interview, and I hand off the camera to Jon for

In the Unarius Reading Room

a minute so I can go fetch the tripod from the car. As I leave, I take *Preparation for the Landing* on the off chance that the Unariuns decide to be less generous. Safely stowed in the car, I think that that's $30 more that will stay in our pockets.

Inside, Jon sits at the head of the table and Frank sits to his left. I wait for Carol to join them, but she won't let us film her. Her hair's a mess and she's not wearing make-up, she claims. I roll tape on Jon and Frank, Carol sitting safely out of sight. Jon starts with Frank, asking how he got involved in Unarius.

"My first interest is in spacecraft," he says. "My memories of space travel caused a lot of inquiry as a youngster, then gradually, as people didn't really relate to that—the prop plane was the most advanced form of travel in my youth—it sort of slipped away. But as time went on, we had things called Blue Book Project and a few other things, and of course the trip to the moon, and various things like that all kind of kept me perked along." In 1974, he received a flyer in the mail for a UFO convention in Anaheim, Calif., and it immediately took his interest. The airplanes and Apollo missions seemed clumsy to him, he says: "I always felt that there was another way. So therefore, when *this* hit–a convention for UFOs–wow, that was right on target.

"Little did I know that I was going to meet the one that we know as Uriel," says Frank, "–Mrs. Norman, cofounder of the Unarius Academy of Science. From that point on, it was just getting acquainted with another language, which was more logical and sensible than the life I was leading. At that event, in a lecture with other scientists there from NASA and so on, Mrs. Norman–who we know as Uriel– spoke on behalf of energy and life on other worlds in the most sensible and logical way. And I said, 'Now, that sets it.'" Frank soon learned that she was the cofounder of Unarius, and began to make trips to El Cajon to read the literature and take classes. By 1978, he had moved here permanently to be close to the Center and be more involved.

Frank Sarlock, student of Unarius

Jon turns his attention to Carol, asking her to describe her experience, and I'm left to find something to shoot. I focus on Jon for a bit, but that's not too interesting since Carol's doing all the talking right now. Finally, I scan the bookshelves and paintings in the background, settling on a Hellenic statuary in the background. The firm-jawed figure stands in for Carol.

"I was living at the time in the back hills of North Carolina, building a shelter—a house," the disembodied voice says. "My daughter had heard Uriel speaking on the radio, and we wrote for information, as many people do." I presume that this happened while Mrs. Norman was still among the living, although considering the nature of many of Unarius's communications, I might be jumping to conclusions. "When I read the information," Carol continues, "it rang something in me that said, 'this is what I'm looking for.' I had been on a search through all of the metaphysical literature I could get my hands on, and it was like finding something that I had been looking for and knowing that that was it. Suddenly I could stop my search. It united all of the teachings that I had read before. It was as if you had many different religions and they all have a common source. And yet, in the telling of the story of the religion, it has changed, each one taking a slightly different course. And yet I always knew there was this truth behind it all. And that's what I found."

Eight years ago, Carol, too, moved to El Cajon, to work and learn. "Unarius is a teaching center, and therefore first efforts here are classes that are conducted every Wednesday, Friday, and Sunday," she says. Unarius also publishes books—more than 100 titles so far—and produces video programming in its studio: "Some psychodrama, some documentary," says Carol, "that are aired on public access cable throughout the country. Our new video cablevision guide is now available."

Being channeled to a channel near you.

Jon asks about 2001, and the arrival. "We do have communication from those who are living on higher dimensional worlds and also those who will be coming," says Carol.

"Their main purpose will be to help mankind solve numerous problems?" asks Jon.

"Oh, yes," Frank says emphatically, "that's the idea." I swing the camera back to Frank, relieved to have an animate subject. "In fact," he continues, "we have the advance knowledge here in our library, which we've stored for the people of the planet Earth. There are a

How we'll always remember Carol Robinson

number of devices to help us to get over the various difficulties, both physical and mental. Primarily mental, because everything really stems from that, and all the terrible shocks that people have gone through and then re-go through. Life repeats; history repeats itself." Unarius teaches that reincarnation and karma are both real, and the cause of problems in your current life. "What can we do to overcome this?" Frank asks rhetorically. "Well, we have to discover who we are and what part we played in the past. So past-life therapy becomes a very, very important part of the understanding of energy."

"Karma really is cause and effect," adds Carol. "We, as we live, experience many of the effects of the karma that we created in the past. Really, it's saying that we set in motion—in our lives in the past—experiences, traumas, and events that now are affecting us as that energy has returned. And, as all energy travels in cycles, we reexperience the energy of our past actions. And that really is what karma is. Our task in understanding our own consciousness is to gain perspective on that energy that we expressed before, deciding anew the value of it in our lives, and if it was negative, to reexpress that energy in a positive sense this time. In doing that, we work with the very essence of our being, and therefore can incarnate in the future with much reduced karma because we have learned the lessons that we have come to have to know."

From the Unarius literature, I recall one student's testimonial that gives an insight:

"Ever since our daughter was old enough to

work, she has not been able to keep a job ... so one day I made an attunement with my higher self and questioned whether I was responsible for her condition. A picture was shown of a former lifetime that explained my dilemma.

"My daughter and my present husband were married and I was their daughter. I was very jealous of their closeness and deeply hated my mother. I became insanely angry and shot her from behind. The bullet did not kill her, but crippled her and she became a quadriplegic ... I now understand that I am totally responsible for her inability to find a job.

"As a result of my realization, in two weeks she had a job and began paying all her bills! I am so appreciative to my spiritual teacher, Uriel, for helping me solve this problem."

"So you don't rely on any outside individual or other place," says Frank. "Everybody's connected. It's a matter of choice to become aware of this infinite contact that you have. And this way, it makes one person feel that 'I can be responsible for my actions. I can overcome.'"

Past-life therapy turns up a lot of things. For starters, you find out that you used to be a bunch of famous people. And then you discover those people weren't what everyone thinks they were. According to the literature, Ernest Norman was once Jesus of Nazareth. Ruth Norman was the 13th Apostle, Mary of Bethany. You don't remember her? She was Jesus's wife, and the author of the Book of

Revelations (the one we all know as "The Revelation to *John*," mind you). In her other lifetimes, Ruth has been Socrates, Peter the Great, Charlemagne, Queen Elizabeth I, Queen Maria Theresa, Hatshepsut, Akbar of India, Quetzalcoatl (a winged serpent god?), and Atahualpa, the last Inca of Peru. And then she became Ruth Norman, truly, the greatest of all these figures.

Their past identities aren't all that the Normans uncovered. The grand scheme of Earth's history has also been revealed, and the truth about Atlantis. About 12,000 years ago, the Atlanteans landed on our planet and set up their beautiful, technologically advanced cities on a continent in the Atlantic Ocean. Unarius's literature is somewhat sketchy on the details here, but it seems that the Atlanteans didn't share their goodies with the natives of Earth. Some of the aboriginal earthlings tried to steal their technology, and in their great envy, succeeded in using it to blow the continent of Atlantis right to the bottom of the sea. Ernest Norman's descriptions of these events, and those of the future, have an unpleasant, racist undertone:

> "Atlantis was blown into oblivion by the very power that it generated, wrongly used in the hands of ignorant black people who sought to rule the world. Again in our present day, could the racial strife in America and other countries be a psychic remanifestaion of the destruction of the world more than 12,000 years ago?..."
>
> "The people of tomorrow will have undreamed of luxuries and conveniences, a way of life which

will exceed even the most fantastic science fiction stories; yet will our present-day mankind be able to survive? Indeed not. The homogeneous mixture of races presents a far too low state of mentality, a heterogeneous society torn and twisted with strictures and rent by irreparable schisms.

"It is quite safe to predict in that future, should it ever arrive, the breed of man who will occupy it will be vastly different than those presently now living—a comparison to the golden-skinned Atlanteans in their beautiful highly-scientific society which, through its egregious philosophy, permitted the dark-skinned ones to overpower and destroy the world. And is it not apparent that in this time history is beginning to repeat itself?"

The power that destroyed Atlantis will someday power our own society. For the Atlanteans had a magnificent power-generating structure that somehow pulled energy right out of the higher spiritual dimensions. What did this structure look like? Why, a pyramid, of course. Which is why the Egyptians built theirs, to try to duplicate, in stone rather than metal, the destroyed originals. The Atlantean pyramids haunt us today, not only in the sands of Egypt, but also in inventions which, Unarius insists, were based on psychic echoes of the Atlantean devices. Take Nikola Tesla's Tesla Coil, which can transmit electricity through the air (as could the Atlantean Pyramids). Unarius claims that Tesla was also on the verge of tapping into an inter-dimensional power source just before he died.

It would be well if he had solved such problems, not just for the benefit of limitless, free energy, but also to understand certain "supernatural" phenomena, leftovers from Atlantis that plague us. "You've heard of the Bermuda Triangle?" Frank asks Jon. "That's the reason for the landing being in that area. There is a generator from Atlantis that is broken, so to speak, but yet is operating in a random sense. Since it works off the very principles of interdimensional energy, if it's at random, a ship or plane going in that area at a particular time—not a regular time, but at a particular time—could disappear because of the tremendous energy." In 2001, he adds, the Muon scientists who land will work with our own scientists to repair the generator, giving us a harmless, limitless power source. "And that's what this ship is," he says, "an advance ship before the ships from the Interplanetary Confederation. Which is the real purpose of all this: to get prepared. And this is one of the preparatory efforts."

Our own power solutions, such as nuclear fission, have caused great distress to beings on the other planets of the Interplanetary Confederation. As Alta (of Planet Vixall), the Interplanetary Ambassador for the 33 Worlds, has channeled to Unarius:

> "You have come to the point, in your scientific technology, where you are tapping the atom in such a way as to cause its distortion. You are disrupting the regular isochronal pulse beat of this atom, and as a result, you are generating an out of phase beat frequency, resulting in disease,

affecting worlds which are distant from yours, worlds of great numbers of people."

Alta further writes: "The phrase 'extraterrestrial phenomenon' will change when it is understood that terrestrial beings are not necessarily 'extra' nor are they a phenomenon!" It points out one of the ways that Unarius is not quite in sync with the rest of the UFO community. Some things are similar: flying saucers, warnings that humanity has been shut off from and spiritually out of tune with the rest of the universe ("No wonder, then, that your planet has been known by many different names: the Dark Planet, the Insane Planet of the Robots."–Alta of Vixall), news of an increase in alien visibility, and a humanoid alien species from the Pleiades star cluster (the Muons of Myton). But other elements of Unarius's story have a different outlook.

First, all aliens are human beings. There are no other intelligent species, which is why the Atlanteans fit in so well with the rest of us and why we should feel such an affinity towards the rest of the universe's population.

The Grays? Well, they may be the most well-known UFOnauts in popular culture, but they don't figure as largely in the Unarius picture. Unarius does have an explanation, Frank tells us: The Grays are actually robots. These robots are psychically linked to humans on distant planets, so that they are, in effect, surrogate visitors to Earth, the eyes and ears of those who are smart enough not to endanger themselves by visiting us in person just yet.

Alien abduction, as far as I can tell, doesn't seem to fit

into Unarius at all. In fact, the whole psychology of abductees is something foreign to the Unarius philosophy. As abduction researcher Budd Hopkins notes, abductees experience something which is the opposite of religion—all miracles, no explanations, and participants who want to disbelieve what is happening. Unarius, though, has no mysteries; all is explained through Unarius.

Their research and documentation is exhaustive. Unarius not only claims that Earth is going to become the 33rd member of the Interplanetary Confederation, but they have descriptions of the other 32 worlds and their inhabitants. Many of the planets were in distress before the Archangel Uriel made contact to convince them of the true nature of the universe and encourage them to form the Confederation. On Ballium, the people had become enslaved by their own labor-saving machines. Other worlds, like Osnus and Endinite, were ravaged by war; the people of Osnus had to move underground from a lack of surface air, while the Endinites, poisoned by atomic explosions, became mutants with four arms and one eye. Other humans with a somewhat different appearance are the people of Dal, whose skin is blue. Unarius even gives an unbiased description of Earth, noting that "Ruth Norman is the planet's great, World Teacher in the consciousness of URIEL, a Prince of the Realm of the Seventh dimension of the Causal Worlds." Little did we know.

We wrap up the interview, and Frank invites us to this October's 13th Annual Interplanetary Conclave of Light Symposium, a strange gathering with classes, lectures, films, a message channeled live from Alta of Vixall, and a parade where—"accompanied by the music of the spheres"—33 people march, each with a pastel-colored flag representing one of the planets of the Confederation. We tell him we'll see what we can do, and silently thank our guardian Archangels that we'll be 3,000 miles away.

As I carry the tripod and camera out to the car, I gaze at the enormous mural beside the parking lot and think of the future—getting some lunch, this afternoon's drive toward Las Vegas, Nev., and the seemingly not-too-distant year 2001. A mere five years from now, it promises to be a time of big change—if Unarius is right. Atlantis will rise from the sea. The first of the spaceships will land openly. Limitless power, world peace, and universal brotherhood will all follow. And we'll all have to wear pastels.

On the surface, Unarius doesn't seem all that bad. The Unariuns place the blame for your problems on your own head (even though it was during a different lifetime) and encourage taking responsibility for and control over your own life. Their philosophy is extremely inclusive (even though the racial thing strikes a discordant note) and claims salvation for all, damnation for none. Why, even if we don't believe what they're saying, they don't care. Actually, it doesn't seem that we need to be prepared for the landing—it's going to happen anyway, and we'll be none the worse afterward for not believing (unlike most millennial-minded religions, for whom only the devout are safe). They genuinely want to educate people and don't seem to be running some cultist brainwashing money scam. Membership is only $75 annually, and their books aren't outrageously priced ($6 for a paperback, $18

Ruth Norman, Cosmic Visionary

or $20 for most hardcovers). And, of course, they were more than generous with us, sending me literature and giving us *Preparation for the Landing* for free.

The flipside, though, is the quality of what you're paying for. *Preparation* isn't one for the *Times* bestseller list. And, of course, much of the pseudoscience they're pushing is completely unfounded and sometimes laughable. But the most dangerous thing about Unarius is what will happen if they're right.

If Unarius is wrong, oh well. They'll close up shop, or, more likely, will say that the Muons had car trouble and won't be able to get here until 2025. But if they're right, then the future may become a scary place. Writing standards will crumble as unedited, channeled works flood the marketplace. Seven hundred years of advancements in the understanding of perspective, color, and light will be cast aside in favor of purple oceanscapes painted by artists who were previously (and thankfully) unknown even to themselves. Any objective view of science and history will be lost. And, most horrifying, everyone will start wearing pastel robes and carrying magic wands.

Unarius has all the answers to the problems of the 20th century; it's a cultural revolution on the brink of release. But quite frankly, if world peace, the truth about extraterrestrials, and cosmic harmony must come at such a price, I'd just as soon keep wearing jeans and a black T-shirt, writing merrily away in ignorance on a dark, insane, pastel-hating planet.

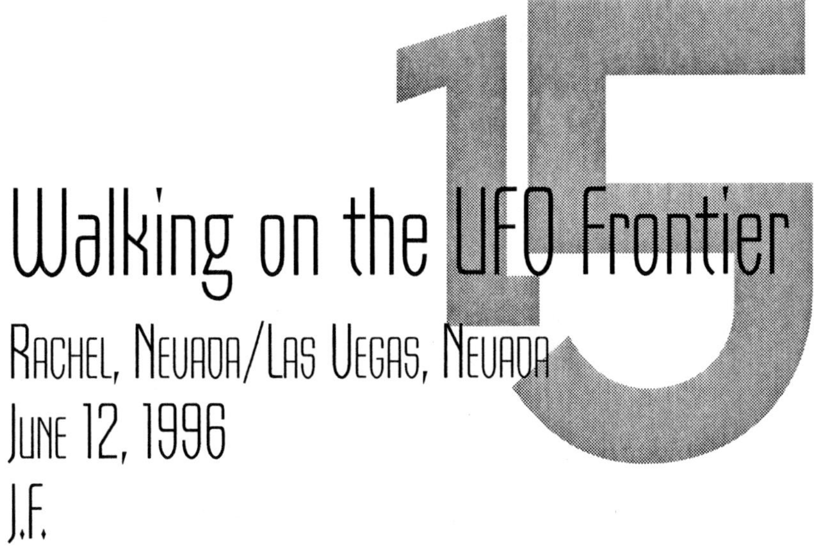

Walking on the UFO Frontier

Rachel, Nevada/Las Vegas, Nevada
June 12, 1996
J.F.

The Little A'Le'Inn's walls are coated with a thick skin of UFO culture. Blurry shots of glowing objects in the night sky, posters of friendly extraterrestrials, and pictures of UFO researchers are pinned, taped, and otherwise thrown together in a mish-mash collage. I stare at my under-cooked barbecued chicken and wonder if we've made a mistake. This back-country combination bar/diner/gift shop/motel is the only sign of civilization for more than fifty miles in either direction down Highway 375.

We're in Rachel, Nev., within spitting distance of the least-secret secret base in the world: Area 51. The region surrounding this military installation has long been noted for lights in the sky, nighttime activity thought by many to be evidence of extraterrestrial intelligence. Tonight,

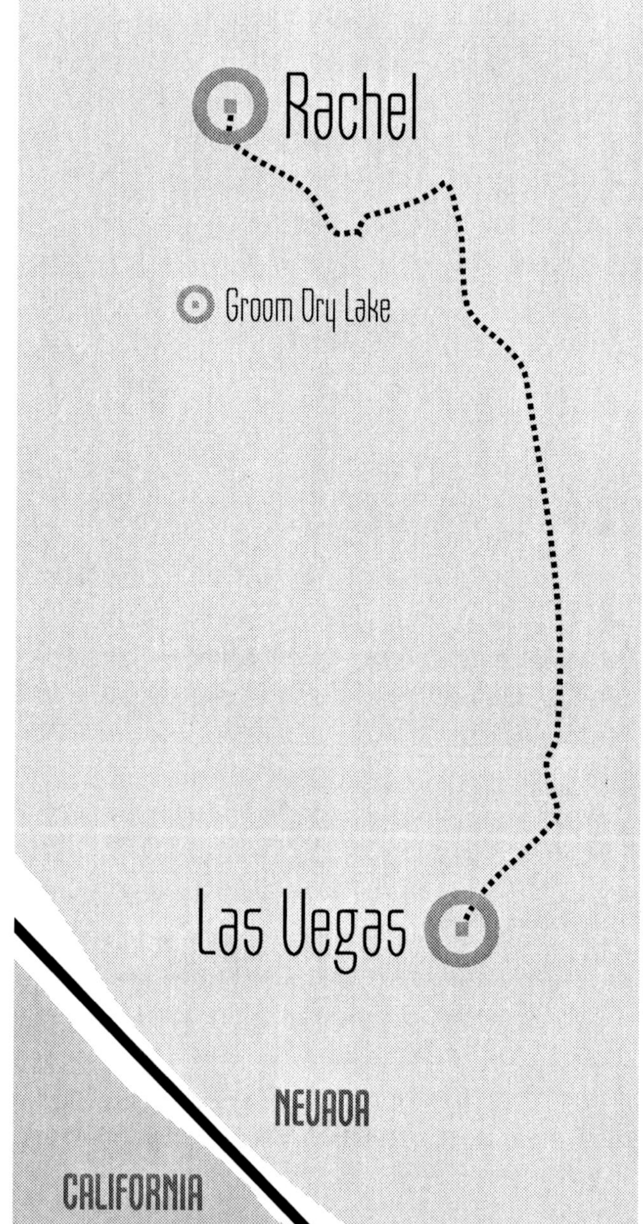
Rachel
Groom Dry Lake
Las Vegas
NEVADA
CALIFORNIA

Matt and I will hike to Tikaboo Peak, a mountain that overlooks the base, in the hopes of seeing a flying saucer.

The origins of the current UFO bustle in Rachel can be traced to 1989, when Bob Lazar appeared on a Las Vegas CBS affiliate, claiming to be a physicist previously employed by the U.S. government to "reverse engineer" recovered flying saucers. According to Lazar, this project was housed at S-4, a top-secret military installation located in the dry bed of Papoose Lake, just south of Area 51. Area 51 and S-4 share the same airspace, which can be clearly seen from Highway 375. Lazar's claims opened the tourist floodgates, and since 1989, sky gazers by the thousands have come to the town of Rachel in the hopes that they might see something outerworldly.

Calling this collection of trailers misplaced in the Nevada desert a "town" is being generous. However, the dusty scenery and rugged living conditions aside, Rachel

An alien oasis

UFO culture at the Little A'Le'Inn

has an interesting story to tell. Simply put, the UFO phenomenon has split Rachel into rival factions. There are
those, like Pat and Joe Travis, the Little A'Le'Inn's owners,
who are sure that our planet has been visited by alien
beings from another world. And there are those, like Area
51 researcher Glenn Campbell, who are still waiting for
more solid evidence. Even though a civil war doesn't
seem imminent between the two factions, it's clear that
no one's willing to give an inch. The truth has been spoken; the line has been drawn in the sand; and Glenn
Campbell has been banished from the Little A'Le'Inn.

Matt and I peruse the odd shamble of shelves that
serves as the Inn's gift nook, located in the far right cor-
ner by the bar. I find nothing that interests me among the
overpriced tourist bait, but Matt gives in and buys a green
alien candle for his brother.

"You gonna check out the base?" the Inn's bartender
asks us.

"That's the plan," Matt replies.

"Then you should talk to Chuck," the bartender says,
pointing his thumb towards a nondescript fellow wearing

jeans and a baseball cap. Chuck, whose advice to us is limited to a grunt of acknowledgment, is an Area 51 and S-4 researcher. In pursuit of the truth, Chuck has pulled a few boneheaded stunts, including driving down Groom Lake Road and crossing the border into the air base's clearly marked restricted zone—which often gets people arrested. Chuck's theories place him safely in the pro-alien camp along with Mr. and Mrs. Travis.

Seeing that Chuck is otherwise occupied, we thank our hosts for our mediocre dinner and head out into the dying heat of dusk in the Nevada desert. As we slide into the car I notice a stone monument to the film *Independence Day,* which stands in front of the Inn like a weird pagan idol. It seems that even Hollywood has a foot in Rachel. *Independence Day* isn't scheduled for release until July 4, and this garish advertising can only be intended for visitors like Matt and myself.

Worship Independence Day.

It's now official.

Between the *Independence Day* idol and the "Extraterrestrial Highway" 375, newly christened by Nevada's state government, it doesn't surprise me that Pat and Joe Travis will stake their lives on the presence of aliens in this nowhere place. Space beings or no, it has been lucrative for them to do so. Unless you're a UFO enthusiast or a reporter, there's no reason to be anywhere near Rachel. UFO tourism is big business here; perhaps, the only business here, and the Little A'Le'Inn's only competition is Glenn Campbell's slightly less flying-saucer-friendly Area 51 Research Center.

On the other side of the Area 51 security border, in an equally self-serving scenario, the United States government refuses to acknowledge the existence of the air base that has given birth to the Stealth Bomber and a host of similar black budget projects. The government will admit to having "facilities" at Groom Lake, the dry bed in which the base is located, but nothing more. They can't deny that these "facilities" are extremely important to them, however. Area 51 is jealously protected. Put your big toe just one inch over the border onto government land, and you'll quickly find yourself detained, searched, and fined heavily by camo-clad security men, who, by the way, don't officially exist.

On April 10, 1995, the Air Force withdrew 4,000 acres of Nevada public land from the Bureau of Land Management to protect the mysterious Groom Lake "facilities." Citing reasons of public safety, they took parcels of land which included mountain viewpoints Freedom Ridge and White Sides. From these locations visitors could watch the operations at the base, which was, no doubt, making the Air Force very nervous.

Tikaboo Peak, our destination tonight, is promoted by Groom Lake researcher Glenn Campbell as a prime site for spying on Area 51. It's one of the last viewpoints accessible to the public and not one that's particularly easy to get to. Fortunately, as a part of his *Area 51 Viewer's Guide*, Glenn provides detailed directions to Tikaboo and a description of the trail up the mountain. Because of the sensitive nature of his topic, Glenn is particularly safety-minded. The *Viewer's Guide* is filled with pithy advice like "Do not cross the border," "Do not drive on rougher roads than your car can handle," and "Be prepared for desert extremes." My personal favorites are Campbell's "YOU WILL DIE" warnings which notify inexperienced hikers of the dangers they could encounter when venturing up the mountain. Losing the path, freezing, and getting struck by lightning are all possibilities. Glenn doesn't take Tikaboo lightly. To avoid any legal nastiness, he disavows, in writing, any personal responsibility for injury caused by misinformation he may have inadvertently provided. In his own words, "You're on your own." Matt and I find this

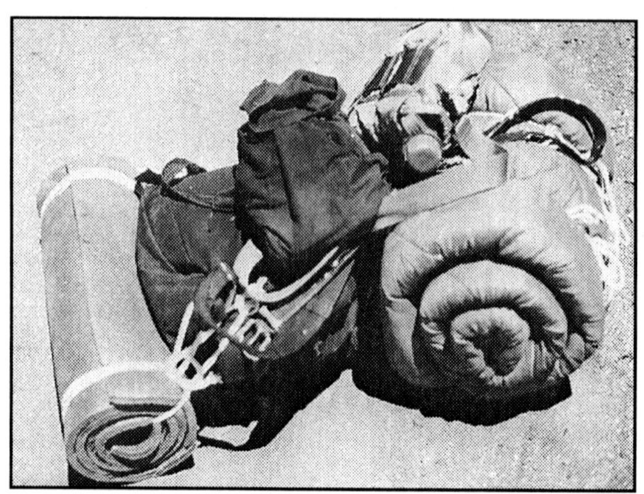

Forty pounds of gear

vaguely reassuring. We didn't travel two thousand miles just for bad barbecued chicken.

Following Glenn's directions to Tikaboo, we drive about 23 miles along a rough dirt road stopping every few miles or so to clear away large rocks that block our path. At 8:15 P.M., we park a half mile from the base of the mountain. The sun is setting, and the air has become pleasantly cool. We gather our camping supplies and canteens, then strap on our backpacks. A quick glance in the car's side mirror reveals the truth: Carrying nearly 40 pounds of gear each, we look like large, brown, misshapen desert turtles. We say good-bye to Matt's Geo and start down the last half mile of road, which is impassable to any vehicle save a good 4×4.

We've decided not to bring the Hi-8 video or the 35mm camera up the mountain with us. Matt and I are in over our heads here, and we know it. According to Campbell's on-line newsletter, *The Desert Rat,* there have been numerous incidents where Campbell and the reporters and photographers accompanying him to view the base have been detained by the Lincoln County Sheriff's Department, which often assists Area 51 security. In many of these cases, the officers searched both the persons and the vehicles of the detained individuals, confiscating any film and video they found. The seized film was then, more often than not, turned over to the Air Force and never seen again. In one incident, Campbell and two journalists from the *New York Times Magazine* were buzzed by a Black Hawk helicopter, presumably piloted by someone from Area 51 security. In another, an ABC News crew on assignment for "World News Tonight with Peter Jennings" had their equipment and videotape taken by Sheriff's deputies. And, in yet another, Glenn was arrested by a Sheriff's deputy while attempting to prevent a videotape seizure from a news crew working for KNBC-TV, Los Angeles.

By the time we reach the base of the trail, the sun has burnt itself out. Matt and I stop to consider our options. We had planned to reach the peak by nightfall but here we are, nowhere near the top, looking at a pitch-black sky. In the *Viewer's Guide,* Glenn specifically warns visitors not to attempt the Tikaboo climb at night, and we don't doubt the validity of his warning. Obviously, dangerous, unfamiliar terrain is that much more dangerous and unfamiliar in the dark. However, we have no intention of driving the three hours back to Vegas, and we can't stay at the Little A'Le'Inn because it's full. We decide to march on. I jokingly suggest we keep our eyes peeled for Grays with abduction on their oversized minds.

We soon come upon a clearing where four paths converge into a well trodden center circle. The yellow orbs of our flashlight beams play off identity-less rocks and trees as we hopelessly search for signs of direction. The paths look so disturbingly similar to each other that we're unsure of which one to take. I become frustrated, angry, then fearful. Our adventure, just barely begun, appears to be at an end. Fortunately, Matt is able to determine our position by the first stars of the evening. Relieved as I am, I still regret making that abduction joke.

We begin climbing, and I scramble over piles of broken rock, grabbing ahold of the occasional tree or large boulder with my gloved hands. My footing is unsure, and I slide and stumble. After a few minutes of struggling, my breath comes in short gasps. I curse and swear and spit. The path becomes so steep that we have to bend nearly double to make any forward progress. We press on, stopping occasionally to drink water greedily from our canteens. My chest burns, my back begins aching, and my legs feel weak. Just as I am about to reach the limits of my endurance, we arrive at the top. The climb up the mountain has taken us almost three hours. We dump our packs and dance for joy. Aliens, we are here.

We set up a tent at Tikaboo's lower campsite, build a fire, and eat cold Chef Boyardee ravioli dinners. We stare at the sky. No UFOs. No flying saucers. Not a thing to be seen. Disappointed, I finish my meager meal and crawl into my sleeping bag. I'm exhausted and, at this point, unwilling to spend the rest of the night gazing at the stars.

Matt has more perseverance than I do, waking up at 5:30 A.M. to watch the base and scan the sky again for UFOs. As he makes a rough sketch of Area 51 in his notebook, he hears jet noise overhead. He looks up to see the gray-green belly of a Stealth Bomber overhead. The bomber is accompanied by a red-and-white fixed-wing escort plane, which Matt supposes is the aircraft that's making all the noise. In a matter of two minutes, the planes disappear into the southwestern sky, heading towards S-4. They make a half-dozen passes during the

The road to Tikaboo Peak

course of the next three hours, all of which I miss. I don't wake up until 9:00 A.M. Whether or not I want to admit it, my body's been totaled by the hike.

I eat a granola bar for breakfast and join Matt on his outcropping perch. As Glenn warned in his *Viewer's Guide,* the Groom Lake base is very far away. We find it difficult to see, even with binoculars. At best, we can identify a few intersecting roads that crawl their way along the desert floor to a conglomeration of dark-colored boxes in the distance. So much for Area 51, America's last remnant of the Cold War.

We investigate the upper campsite and are shocked to find it in a state of complete disarray. Graffiti promoting Chuck Clark's *Area 51 and S-4 Handbook* is scrawled on every smooth surface. A pile of campers' garbage—half-used propane tanks, water bottles, empty cans of food, and a sleeping bag—has been tossed on the fire circle. There is no sign of Glenn Campbell's shrine dedicated to "Our Lady of the Black Budget" except for a few small melted figures lying pathetically on the pile of garbage. A piece of PVC pipe with the words "AREA 51 + S4 HANDBOOK BY CHUCK CLARK BANNED AT THE AREA 51 RESEARCH CENTER" written on it, lies across the top of the heap. Chuck Clark's card is nailed to one of the railroad ties that has been dragged to the peak to provide seating.

Matt and I clean the campsite as best we can, removing the graffiti with a hatchet and our bare hands. We dump the vandalized rocks down the mountain, remove the business card, and take the PVC pipe to use as a walking stick. We have neither the space in our packs nor the energy in our bodies to carry all the garbage down.

Naked in the daylight, the trail appears much more treacherous than it did the night before. It is horrifyingly steep, a desert roller coaster covered with small rocks. Matt and I stare at it, feeling a mixture of amusement and fear. Had we realized the danger yesterday, we would not have attempted the climb during the night. Fortunately, the hike down is much less arduous, even fun. I extend my right leg in front of me and surf over the tumbling gravel, letting the stones take me where they will. We complete the journey in about an hour.

As we reach the last section of the path, we encounter another group on their way up. The party consists of a man and three boys, presumably his sons, who seem less than prepared to take on Tikaboo. The oldest son, about high-school age, looks physically able to handle the hike. However, the father, sporting a baby blue "Stealth Fighter" T-shirt, is carrying not only a giant backpack but a sizable beer gut, as well. The two younger boys, who appear to be about age five, are toting small bottles of Gatorade. We talk to the father for a moment and ascertain that he and his sons are indeed the UFO tourists for whom Glenn has constructed his "YOU WILL DIE" warnings. "I hope we have enough water," the father says worriedly. "I doubt you do," I think as we leave them behind and head for our car.

We stop in Alamo, Nev., for lunch at a Tex-Mex diner. In order to reach the restaurant, we are forced to walk through a gift shop filled with cheap, Nevada tourist merchandise—not that the Trail of Shameless Capitalism is worth the effort. On the other side, the diner greets us

three weeks
worth of
DUST

three weeks

worth of

DUST

96○612

with decor as garish as pink stretch pants. Once a Chinese restaurant, the eatery has fallen to new owners, who apparently can't be bothered to redecorate or even repaint the place. Statues of Chinese lions and red leather booths match poorly with the beef-n-barbecue cuisine—no matter, we think, as long as the food is good. We order quesadillas for an appetizer and learn our culinary lesson well: The down-home Nevada desert chefs cook food that tastes even worse than supermarket brand, family-size Salisbury steak frozen dinners. Between the Little A'Le'Inn and this joint, Matt and I are lucky our stomachs haven't exploded. We choke down our burgers with the super-sweet, cough-syrupy cola and beat a hasty retreat.

We drive back to the Little A'Le'Inn for one more visit before we leave Rachel. Joe Travis, an old guy with a streaked gray beard, is tending bar for two fellows with British accents. One of the Englishmen happens to be a writer freelancing for British *GQ*; it seems that everyone's doing a piece on Area 51. I find it funny that there are now more reporters than locals in this hick-town pub. Joe Travis livens up the afternoon by telling us tall tales about his drunk driving exploits. Apparently, Joe is a cautious drunkard who never speeds. The only time he was ever caught, he claims, is when an officer pulled him over for driving too slowly on the highway. Joe also throws in a conspiracy theory involving King James I, the monarch responsible for the King James translation of the Bible, to entertain his British guests. Matt and I shoot photographs of Joe Travis and the Inn's interior before hitting the road.

Our next stop is the Area 51 Research Center, the mobile home from which Glenn Campbell bases his operations in Rachel. The Research Center is a squat building with a number of television antennae protruding from its roof and a satellite dish out back. During the week, when Glenn is in Vegas, the Center is run by his assistant, Sharon Singer, who, lucky for us, happens to be there when we arrive. The Center sells books, T-shirts, souvenirs, and helpful equipment, like binoculars, with which to spy on the government.

A yellow kitchen counter, cabinets, and drying dishes in

The fruits of Area 51

the rack by the sink remind me that this was once, and perhaps still is, someone's house. Sunlight pours in through the blinds above the sink. Perpendicular to the counter is a black desk with a computer and a conglomeration of papers stacked upon it. A smaller printer table with a phone on it stands nearby, and a classic suburban-style chandelier that looks as if it should be lighting a kitchen table dangles over the desk.

Sharon is a friendly woman in her late twenties or early thirties with blonde hair, tanned skin, and a few red blemishes on her face, wearing a red-and-white striped short-sleeve shirt and denim shorts. She doesn't seem to mind talking with us as she sits in front of the computer.

"Have you gotten to take a look at Area 51?" I ask.

"Yeah," she replies, "I went up to the Freedom Ridge when it was open to the public."

"That was a better view, I guess, than Tikaboo?"

"Yes, it was. Yeah," she answers.

"Do you get a whole lot of UFO tourists around here?" I query.

"Uh-huh," she says in a Midwestern drawl. "Yeah."

"And most of them are polite and clean up their trash or they're just bumbling—," I start, thinking of the camp site on Tikaboo.

"I don't know if they clean up their trash," she interjects, "but we get a lot of really strange ones."

"What was the strangest UFO tourist you've encountered?" I ask.

"Merlin is," she begins, then changes gears. "I guess he qualifies for more than just a tourist. He's been out several times. He is Ambassador Merlin from Draconis."

"So he's from another planet?"

"He is an alien. As he says," she says.

"Does he have any proof of his alienness?" I ask.

"He's got his business card," she says and laughs.

"So, if you're an alien, you carry a business card?" I ask, chuckling as well.

"Yeah, sure," she says, sarcastically.

"Hmm. That's interesting. I've got a business card, but I don't think I'm an alien. I mean, some people may disagree, but ...," I joke.

We say good-bye to Sharon and journey to our last stop in this part of the Nevada desert, the Medlin Ranch black mailbox, a legendary fixture in UFO lore. Because the mailbox is the only man-made object for miles on Highway 375 and relatively close to the military installa-

Hanging out by the black mailbox

Broiled steak, Area-51-style

tions on the other side of the security border, it's a logical gathering point for UFO-minded tourists and sky watchers. Ironically, the black mailbox is no longer black—it's covered with white stencils reminding trespassers that the mailbox is privately owned to discourage vandalism. From a distance the conglomeration of black and white paint makes the mailbox look gray. Perhaps there's a message in this. We investigate the area around the mailbox but find nothing of interest except a dead, bloated cow a few miles distant. Memories of Bovina, Tex., float through my mind, as well as the theories hypothesizing that aliens drink the blood of helpless bovines. However, from the looks of this overinflated cow, not one extraterrestrial has taken even a sip.

We arrive in Las Vegas around 7:00 P.M. and find ourselves a hotel for the night. We're here to talk with Glenn Campbell, the mysterious figure who's been guiding our Area 51 adventure from behind the scenes. Matt and I are unsure of what to expect from Glenn. If knowledge is power, Glenn is certainly the most powerful man in the vicinity of the secret air base. The military has kept tabs on his Internet newsletter and his *Viewer's Guide* to find out just how much the public knows about Area 51. Glenn is a prankster too. He knows he's toying with the U.S. government and enjoys every minute of it. As I drift off to sleep, I imagine Glenn sitting on Tikaboo peak, pulling the strings of interdimensional UFOs and military personnel like some giant puppet master.

We meet Glenn at his apartment the next day. Short, balding, and wearing a short-sleeve tennis shirt, Glenn seems more like a Little League baseball coach than the fearsome, all-knowing god of Area 51. Glenn, however, is endowed with wit, intelligence, and a nonstop, smart-ass sense of humor which more than makes up for his conservative appearance.

"Las Vegas is paradise," Glenn says as we drive into town to get brunch at one of the Shiny City's numerous buffets. Having learned a lesson from our encounter with Leah Haley and Marc Davenport, Matt and I offer to pay for Glenn's meal.

"You guys aren't rolling in it, are you?" he asks.

Matt and I shake our heads no. "Not really," Matt says.

"I can take care of it, then," Glenn says. Apparently, eating and talking with Glenn won't cost us anything.

We pile our plates high with incompatible foods from five countries, then take a seat at a table. Talk wanders to the topic of Las Vegas buffets, on which Glenn is an expert. He has visited almost every smorgasbord in the city and rates them according to selection, rotation, and freshness. Because Glenn has disciplined his stomach to digest food slowly, he requires only one meal a day, which he takes at 11:00 A.M. He refuses to keep any food in his apartment, preferring to eat exclusively in the casinos. Digging into his slice of lemon meringue pie, Glenn stares at his plate with a look of horror.

"I need a vegetable. I forgot a vegetable." Apparently for Glenn, a balanced diet is top priority.

We finish our brunch and drive back to Glenn's apartment, which is located directly across from the Las Vegas Airport. The landing strip nearest his apartment is reserved for planes that fly Area 51 employees to and from the base. "Theoretically," Glenn says, "I could write down license plates."

Glenn's living room is lined with bookshelves containing all sorts of UFO literature. Blueprints of secret military projects adorn the walls: Area 51, the A-bomb. We sit on the couch and chat for awhile.

Glenn tells us how his romance with the U.S. government began. In 1992, he quit his job at a Boston-based software company and headed west to investigate Nevada Highway 375, where it was rumored you could see flying saucers on demand. He didn't find any alien spacecraft, but he did find Area 51, which, all told, was just as good. Glenn began collecting information on the base and recording his activities in his Internet newsletter, *The Groom Lake Desert Rat.*

"In 1993, when I got kicked out of the Little A'Le'Inn, I went down the street and started my own little business. I had to put a sign out front, and I just put 'Area 51 Research Center.' It was a bit of a joke back then, but now it has really taken form. It's a real research center. We collect information on Area 51 and mostly put it on the

Internet for other people to browse," Glenn says.

Has messing with the military made Glenn paranoid? Well, quite frankly, yes. When Glenn printed the first edition of his *Area 51 Viewer's Guide*, he wrote the number 700 on it so that the government would think more copies existed. Fortunately, enough people know about Area 51 now for him to feel a little more secure. Given the amount of attention the secret base has received in the past two years from mainstream television, radio, and print media, Glenn admits his previous precautions now "seem kind of silly."

Besides the relative safety his limited fame as an Area 51 researcher affords, Glenn has reaped other benefits from the popularization of the secret base. He has self-published close to 7,000 copies of the *Viewer's Guide* and has recently acquired a literary agent.

However, as successful as Glenn is now, it would be a

Glenn Campbell basks in the sun.

disservice to him to presume that his early research efforts were without sacrifice, bravery, or ingenuity. Investigating America's last bastion of the Cold War has required Glenn to walk on the frontier. In order to assemble the *Viewer's Guide,* he had to learn to survive in the extreme conditions of the Nevada desert. In order to disperse to the public the information he obtained, he had to become a pioneer publisher on the new medium of the Internet. And, to discover the truth about the air base, he had to face off against a secretive branch of the U.S. government which ignored or dismissed the freedoms associated with conventional American ideology. "Area 51 is like the old Berlin Wall," Glenn says. "It's a place where the totalitarian world meets the free world. There are lots of interesting inconsistencies here."

According to Glenn, because Area 51's security force doesn't officially exist, they don't have to obey civil rights laws or aviation rules. They use illegal methods like "sandblasting" to dissuade overeager Area 51 tourists from approaching the base. "Big military helicopters swoop down on people near the border and blast them good [with sand] to try to get them to leave the area. That's against FAA regulations and the military's own regulations. You're supposed to keep a distance of 500 feet above any object or building. And this is not obeyed."

Because Glenn has done so much painstaking research on Area 51's military activity, he has difficulty believing many of the UFO stories associated with the region. "I've seen plenty of spectacular lights in the sky, but nothing that couldn't be explained as something else: a lens flare, jittery hands, flares, military airplane lights." According to Glenn, the UFO stories that are likely to be true are the much more subtle ones: perhaps Bob Lazar's claim that the government has recovered alien ships and is studying them.

"They say that the government has alien information or has information that it's not giving to the public. I think that that's a very plausible idea and it's very plausible that it would be taking place here, which is our nation's most secure military installation." But Glenn needs solid proof to become a believer.

Finding solid proof has always been difficult for those researchers who work in the UFO field. There is a notable lack of accurate documentation and precise methodology in recording UFO sightings. Bad information based on hearsay is mixed in with good, scientifically based observation, making investigation troublesome. In addition, so many books, articles, videos, and films on the phenomena are produced that it's nearly impossible to find a point where you can wade in safely. Once you do get your feet wet, you have to separate the good and bad data, which can be maddening. And finally, there's the question of what you choose to believe without a shred of scientific knowledge. Like most religious precepts, the idea that UFOs are proof of alien beings more powerful than man requires a bit of faith, at least for now.

"What you have in the UFO field is no rules," Glenn says. "People can believe anything they want to believe and there's no way that you can prove or disprove it. When you have people making decisions for emotional reasons … people will start warring with each other." And that's pretty much the state of UFO research today, in Rachel, Nev., and around the world. Until someone brings an alien home for dinner or people give up and move on to the next big thing, there will be trashed camp sites at Tikaboo peak and a thousand other petty quarrels.

Glenn is disappointed and a little surprised when we mention the state of the Tikaboo camp site. To cheer him up we present him with the piece of graffiti-covered PVC pipe. After all, he got us up and down the mountain safely, and we feel like we owe him a little something in return. It's a gift from the UFO frontier and one we're proud to give. He seems to like it.

Skipping off the Edge of a Cliff

Mount Rainier, Washington
June 19, 1996
M.H.

Mt. Rainier possesses a terrifying beauty. We approach from the west, driving through dense pine forest that, in places, is being thinned and patchily clear-cut by loggers. Beyond this lies the park itself, masked by an even denser, frightfully ancient forest, thick with the growth and debris of millennia. Glimpses of the mountain shoot by through gaps in the trees, but it's not until we're actually on our way up that we get a clear view of the peak. Stark white against a blue June sky, snow whipping off the tip into thin air or cascading down through valleys as a river of powder, the whole damn thing is distracting enough to make me drive right through a guardrail and off a cliff. Whether V-winged craft are skipping about the peak, as Kenneth Arnold claimed they were on June 24, 1947, or

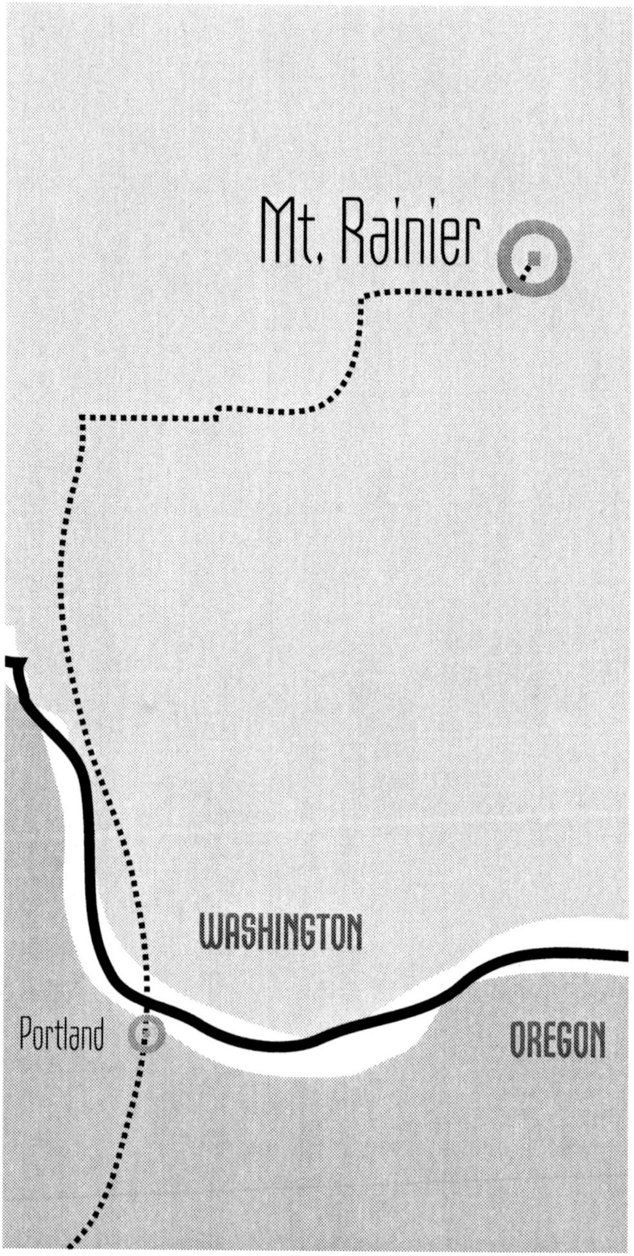

Mt. Rainier
Portland
WASHINGTON
OREGON

not, the lonely mountain is startling enough to look at, and positively dangerous to try to watch while driving.

Every time I glance up to the crystal peak, standing impossibly higher than we are (and we're already thousands of feet above the rocky river fed by the melting snows), I find myself, a moment later, pulling too wide into a surprise curve. The car plays chicken with the guardrail too often to be comfortable, and I have to focus my whole attention on the winding mountain road that, while well-maintained, is nonetheless very, very high up. Very. We swing past the peak and around a wide arc to arrive at a scenic pull-off where I can look at the mountain until I go snow-blind without fear for the rest of my body or car.

Forty-nine years ago next week, Kenneth Arnold's airborne sighting (that is, when *he* was airborne—he was aiding in an aerial search-and-rescue for a downed Marine transport plane) here ushered in the modern age of UFOs. Sure, there had been foo fighters, phantom airships, and

To Mt. Rainier

birthplace

of the

flying

saucer age

birthplace

of the

flying

saucer age

angelic visitations before, but his was the first sighting that received popular press. The sound-bitery of reporter Bill Bequette (or possibly his editors) compressed Kenneth Arnold's description that the objects "flew like a saucer would if you skipped it across the water" into the elegant, somewhat inaccurate, "flying saucer."

A rash of sightings filled out the rest of the summer of 1947, and, whether as a result of the strange nature of UFOs or as a result of Bequette's poetic license, they were all described as disk-shaped. Kenneth Arnold's craft were patently *not* disk-shaped, but rather V-winged, or boomerang-shaped. Still, a boomerang makes for a lousy analogy—one does not imagine a boomerang would skip across a lake as easily as a nice, round kitchen saucer.

Standing at the edge of the cliff, gazing up at the eerie mountain, I can't help but feel a certain sense of awe, and a healthy respect for a positively dangerous piece of geography. The frigid snowcap glacier kills mountain climbers without too much effort. The roads through the park play footsie with massive cliffs that drop off thousands of feet into boulder-strewn rivers. And, as I was constantly reminded while driving for the past two days, reminded by Mt. Shasta in Northern California, reminded by Mt. Hood in Oregon, and smacked upside the head by the enormous, absent chunk of Mt. St. Helens just to the south, Rainier is a volcano, sitting right on the northern end of the good old Ring of Fire. Throw in half a dozen extraterrestrial craft dancing around the summit, and you've got something just freaky enough to make you reconsider taking that cushy multimedia job in Seattle.

Close Encounters and Close Calls

Sand Dunes State Forest, Minnesota
June 22, 1996

17.1 The Creature Emerges from the Forest

M.H.

We've been camping for four days in the dull, under-populated wastes of the American northlands: first in depressed Yakima, Wash., then frosty Montana, featureless North Dakota, and now in the quiet, boring pine forests of Minnesota. After so many weeks on the road, we don't want, or need, to talk to people unless we're interviewing them. We crave no encounters. An alien from outer space would need a pretty good story before we'd feel obliged to take up a conversation with it. Jon and I barely speak now—not from annoyance or anger, but simply because we know there's no need to. We almost never say a word before noon, an agreement that has made getting up less of a chore.

Jon, who's more of a talker than I am, would struggle

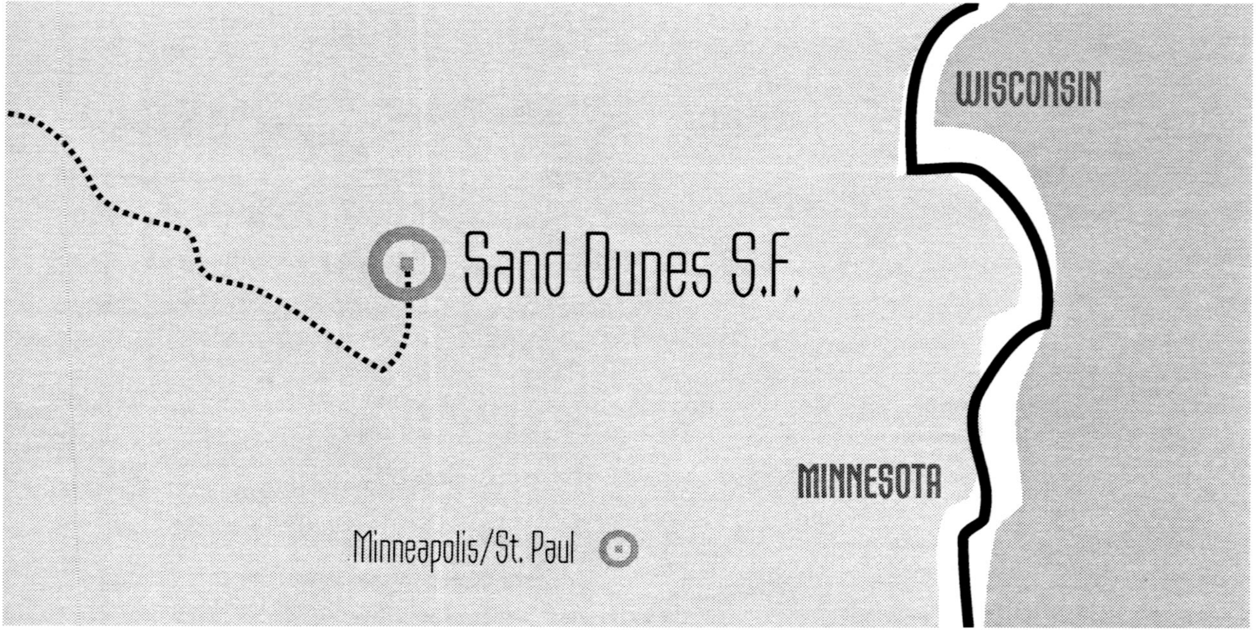

WISCONSIN
Sand Dunes S.F.
MINNESOTA
Minneapolis/St. Paul

through his haze to make conversation as we got ready each day. "You know," I finally told him, "you don't have to talk to me in the morning." It was a revelation—a quiet one. Driving for 12 hours a day, away from other people, with no exposure to popular media, we had effectively removed ourselves from human society. Why carry on its useless conventions? Our days became much smoother.

Thus, when the chubby teenage girl wanders into the light of our campfire, it's more of an intrusion than such a thing would normally be, had we just been out for a fun weekend of camping. She heard Jon practicing his guitar and came to find us. Jon and I, now somewhat beyond speech, size her up in two seconds and share a quick glance that communicates what we both know: This stupid girl is going to be a load of trouble.

She asks if she can join us, and we don't say no. With each word spilling from her soft, round face, my dread

Ann Lake Campground

Our last moments of peace

grows. I can see where it's all heading. She's so glad to meet someone else here at the campgrounds. Even though she's camping with her boyfriend and his friends over there, she says with a wave of her hand, it's pretty boring since she's the only girl.

"Your boyfriend's not going to come over here and beat us up or anything, is he?" Jon asks, and we both laugh a humorless laugh, knowing that he's not joking.

Oh, no, she assures us, giggling—he's not like that at all. Jon and I sit in a nervous calm, listening to her tell us that she's 19, went to one year of community college, dropped out, and is now working for some catalog company. All the teens come here on weekends to drink—until the park rangers come around and take away the beer, of course. That happens a lot.

She turns her pudgy face and community-college, frizzy brown hair towards us and asks, "What are you guys doing here?"

With a sigh and another mutual look, we go into the spiel. We're driving cross-country, visiting famous UFO sites. And so on. She, of course, doesn't know about any of the UFOs that buzzed Sand Dunes State Forest and nearby Elk

River, Minn., back in 1992, but I don't expect her to. Lots of places have rashes of sightings, and even if she was probably less worried about intergalactic travelers and the transformation of the human race than she was about her dreamy first real boyfriend and starting off her underage drinking bright and early at the tender age of 15, I still wouldn't fault her for not having heard about them.

CSETI is what puts this backwater on the map—maybe not the really good maps, but on some map, I suspect. CSETI, the Center for the Study of Extraterrestrial Intelligence, got its start in Minnesota in 1990 and held sky watches here at the park after the 1992 sightings. A loosely knit international organization founded by ER doctor Steven Greer, CSETI attempts to initiate contact with UFOs. The members of CSETI, who spend most of their time waving at the UFOs near Mexico City these days, use deer-spotting flashlights, radar detectors, and mental telepathy to attempt communication with UFOs and their occupants. They claim to have elicited behavioral changes from the craft when they blink their deer-spotters at them, and even say that they have physically met and telepathically communicated with short alien beings in the mountains outside of Mexico City.

Such a coup, a human-initiated contact with a UFO, is classified as a CE-5, says CSETI. The claim, I'm sure, causes concern in nearby Chicago, where CSETI's acronym neighbor, CUFOS—the Center for UFO Studies—dwells. CUFOS was founded by the late J. Allen Hynek, former Project Blue Book chief investigator and coiner of the terms "swamp gas" (which he used to explain the sightings at Ann Arbor, Mich., a conclusion he later recanted), "high strangeness" (an annoyingly overused phrase in UFO literature describing anything that is unbelievably odd, i.e., most of the UFO field), and "close encounter of the (nth) kind." His CE ratings gave some sort of scientific classification to sightings: A CE-1 (close encounter of the first kind) is just a light in the sky. A CE-2 usually involves physical evidence or effects, such as scorched marks on the ground, debris, stalled car engines, or radiation burns. And a CE-3 requires the sighting of a UFO occupant. That's all Hynek laid out. Since then, the higher CE numbers have been fiercely contested by newcomers. A CE-4 usually means that a human being has been aboard a UFO, or has been abducted. And now CSETI wants a CE-5 to mean that we are the ones bothering the aliens. Not that we have any real power to compel them to answer us, it seems. Like some sort of collect call.

Whatever. What it means in Sand Dunes State Forest—a place where the only sand appears to be on the yards-wide lakefront beach—is that the park is just a sentimental sort of place, where one of the more organized goofy factions of UFO research has its roots, and where you can camp out in reasonable peace and stare at the sky on a summer night.

Unless some annoying girl is chatting you up when you only want to be left alone to mull over the last few weeks and let slip the cares of the road and marathon driving. We say hardly anything, but we blow her away. Just the fact that we have driven in a big circle around the country leaves her awestruck. Finally, we feign tiredness and start packing up and getting ready for bed, and she leaves us, letting us know that we're soooooo cool.

A few minutes later, as we put the ice chest and the guitar into the car, she ambushes us with a camera. She wants a picture to remember us by, since we're soooooo cool. And if we get famous, the photos will be worth something. She flashes away at us in the dark, and then goes again, bubbling with joy. Years from now, our faces will share a drawer of some neglected bureau with those of her dear friends, her parents, and her grandchildren. The burden of future years weighs heavy on us, so Jon and I head for the tent and try to sleep.

Then the shouting starts, from over there, in the direction that she waved her chubby little hand by the fireside. We prick up our ears and listen in silence, not believing how accurately we called the night's outcome.

"Where were you?" screams a male voice. A female whine responds.

"When I get back, I expect you to be here!" he shouts back. More female squeaks.

"I don't want you wandering around the woods!" he declares, followed by the question that nails it all into place: "Who were you with?" The female voice is hysterical, obviously denying any wrongdoing, trying to calm him while he rants on.

I reach above my head, into the small pouch on the side of the tent. After I fish around for a few seconds, Jon turns to me and says, "What are you doing?"

"Oh, just looking for Mr. Knife," I say, pulling my pocketknife from the pouch. It seems very small in my hand.

Jon pauses, listening to the shouts, straining to hear any footsteps or snapping twigs.

"Should I get my knife?" he asks, his voice grave, his breathing a bit quicker. When considering protection, we decided it would be a bad idea to bring firearms on the trip (not that we docile white suburbanites even own any in the first place) but figured that carrying a good knife or two would be thoroughly legal and not a bad idea. Jon's survival knife has a curving 5 1/2-inch blade and serrated edge; it's the kind you take into the jungle if you're only allowed to carry one item and you want to come out alive three weeks later. It's also currently in the car.

I consider what poor defensive options a sleeping bag and a nylon tent with one zippered exit offer. Sure, I'm a black belt, but I've luckily never gotten into a fight—and only an idiot would want to fight from inside a bag. "'Might be a good idea," I say. He nods in the dark.

17.2 Paralyzed

J.F.

Certain that the drunken, belligerent rednecks will arrive at any moment, I claw around the bottom of the tent for my boots. I jam them onto my bare feet and hastily tie them up.

The shouts coming from the drunks' camp site are sporadic and awful—lunatic, in fact. I realize that, if the situation heats up, as it looks like it will, I am going to see a great deal of violence up close. I took Tae Kwon Do in high school, and got into a scrap or two as a kid, but fighting, for the most part, is completely foreign to me. I can hear the verbal pissings of the insane boyfriend getting louder and louder.

I push back the tent flap and lunge into the blackness of the forest night. The car, my goal, is only a few yards to the left of the tent. I scamper towards the Geo, slip the key into the lock, and turn it slowly. Click. I open the door and the car's interior lights flash on, certain to attract the attention of the backwoods psychos. I must do this quickly. I reach beneath the front passenger's seat, groping for my hunting knife, a gift from my uncle when I was a teenager. I finally locate the hilt among the debris of McDonald's wrappers, cassette tapes, and road maps piled on the floor. Triumphant, I grab the weapon, slide off the front seat, and close the door. I tuck the weapon into the front pocket of my sweatshirt, treasuring the momentary feeling of relief it brings me. I'll stab those motherfuckers if they come at us. Then, I'm terrified again.

Ever since I was a child, I've had Obsessive Compulsive Disorder, which, in various forms, affects millions of Americans, some more severely than others. I wouldn't say my case is a particularly serious one, but when I get nervous or tense, my OCD gets much, much worse. Basically, I'm a checker. I want to make sure that appliances—stoves, toasters, coffee makers, and the like—are off, and that doors—to cars, apartments, offices, etc.—are locked. I reach to close the car door, and the monster in my head decides it's time to come out and mess with me. I panic. What will happen if the drunks get into our car? Everything we need for this trip is in the car, and if we lose it, we're screwed. I need to make sure the vehicle's locked. I check the car door once, pulling the handle up until it makes a clicking sound. Then I check it again. Click. And again. Click. The cries coming from the drunkards' camp-site are becoming uglier and more frequent. Click. Click. Click. What if they steal our car and crash it? What if they crash it into us? Click. Click. Click. I can't stop checking.

I realize the idiocy of what I'm doing and use all my remaining willpower to calm myself down and force myself to stop checking. I rush towards the tent and almost get there. But, the nagging suspicion that the car is not locked won't leave my head. The monster's not fin-ished with me yet. I have no choice. I have to check the car again. It takes me three or four tries to break free of my own neuroses and finally walk to the tent.

"You were checking weren't you?" Matt whispers from inside. He knows me pretty well.

"Yeah," I reply. "I'm going to hide behind the tent. All right?"

"All right," he says, and I scamper, nervously, around the back. I crouch, positioning myself so I can see whoever might be coming from the drunks' campsite. Now, all I have to do is wait.

17.3 Physical Evidence

M.H.

I strain to make out more details among the not-too-distant shouts. A yard or more behind my head, Jon's breathing is ragged and loud. In the polarized night, where there exists only the teenagers' screams and the utter silence of the rest of the world, Jon's breathing seems deafening—as unmissable as a lighthouse on some moonless shore. They're certain to hear him, I think, and wonder which one of us is in more danger—me, trapped in the tent with no way to escape, or him, exposed and obvious beside the tent.

It's then that the big noise and the bright lights come, drowning out Jon's shallow breathing. Car headlights swing through the trees, and tires crunch gravel as they roll closer—the rangers or the police have arrived. An

In the car, tired and rained-out

The smoking gun

adult voice speaks, a radio crackles, and the boyfriend mouths off to the cop. From snatches of conversation drifting our way, I gather that someone at another campsite used a cell phone to call the cops and complain about the screaming. Everyone is underage, of course, so the cop is going to confiscate the beer. The boyfriend knows it, and in a rare moment of brilliance, decides to outwit the cop by chugging down the last of his beer before it can be taken away.

At this open show of incredibly stupid defiance, a note of finality enters the cop's voice and I hear handcuffs clink and snap as he hauls the idiot off to the police station. The party breaks up pretty quick, and Jon leaves his defensive position behind the tent and comes back in. We fall asleep after the last of the teens' cars pulls away.

The next morning, rain—the first rain yet out of a dozen nights of camping—starts seeping in at the door of our tent and awakens us with wet feet. During a short break in the storm, we roll up the gear, stuff it into the trunk of the car, and get moving a few hours earlier than we had planned. We loop the campgrounds once, pausing at the site that undoubtedly belonged to our tormentors. Empty

212

cans of beer and cheese balls litter the picnic table—phys-ical evidence of our encounter. A CE-2? It wasn't a CE-5, that's for sure—we weren't the ones that initiated contact. And regardless of what Stephen Greer and CSETI hoped they might find in these woods, it is our research that has yielded the final, conclusive results: There is no intelligent life here.

Highway's End?

Dayton, Ohio
June 25, 1996
J.F.

According to UFO lore, when saucers fall from the sky, the U.S. military takes the recovered debris, and in some cases, the alien bodies, to Wright-Patterson Air Force Base in Dayton, Ohio. UFOlogists have, for the past 50 years, cited accounts from workers at this base as evidence to support UFO cover-up and government conspiracy theories. These sources have been at different times both anonymous and named. Perhaps most importantly, UFO investigations conducted by the U.S. government have started and ended here, at the base.

It's appropriate, then, that Wright-Patterson is the final stop on our UFO journey. The U.S. Air Force Museum at the base is open to the public, so Matt and I go there first. Outside the museum, tourists waddle about, necks craned

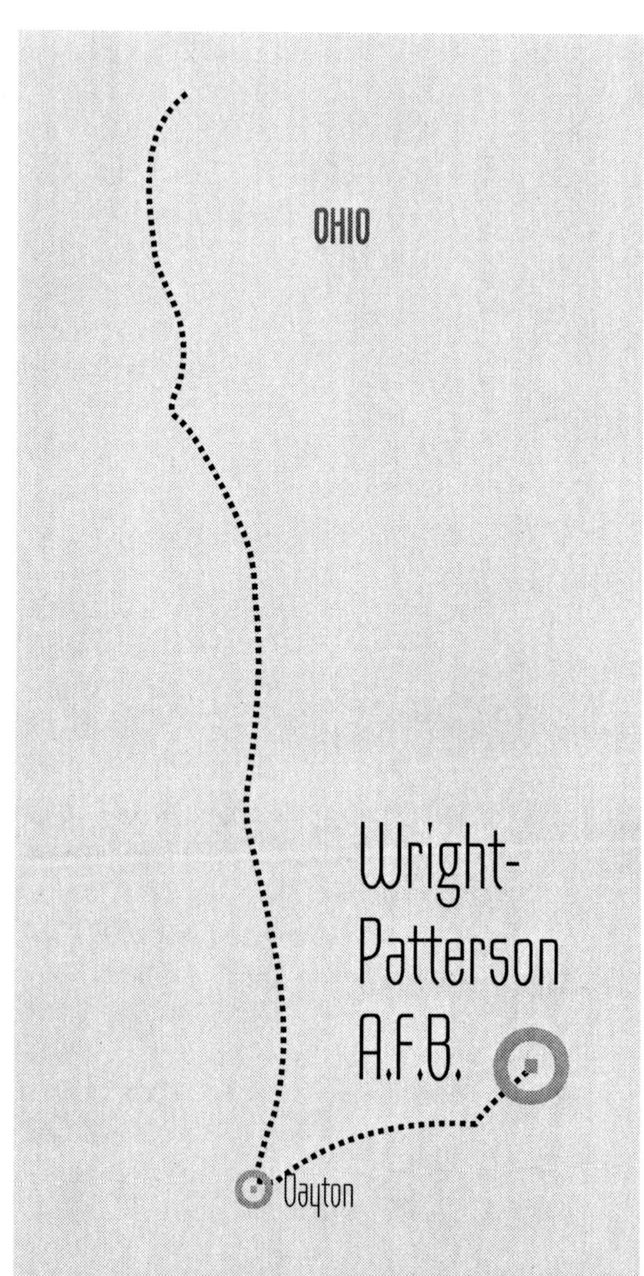

OHIO
Wright-
Patterson
A.F.B.
Dayton

to see the tops of the rockets that rise from the lawn like steel trees. Squat, boxy hangars with curved roofs sit up close to the sidewalk, and a crackling voice over the loudspeakers invites visitors to the Museum lobby to pick up vehicle passes for the Annex building. The voice's offer is appealing. We know that this might be our only chance to see the other parts of the base, to look at the buildings where alien bodies very well could be housed. But this trip has fried our skulls. The road has taken its toll. We decide we will do our investigation here.

There's a fellow selling ice cream from a small white cart on the sidewalk. While the cart doesn't have the same kitschy charm that Mt. Shasta's neo-hippie dessert shop Intergalactic Delights did, it seems like it's worth a look. This adventure has become ridiculous, but I remind myself that we've been on the road for nearly five weeks. The Grays love strawberry, and when you're looking for aliens, everything you see and do takes on UFO connotations.

Here comes the nuke, little darlin'.

Just an ice cream boy

The vendor is a thin, sharp-featured young guy with wire-rim glasses, a crew cut, and a stark white T-shirt. He's sitting under an umbrella, which shades him and the frozen treats from the summer sun. I walk slowly up to the cart.

"Have you seen any aliens or UFO-related activity?" I ask.

"I'm just the ice cream boy," he replies. "They don't really tell you anything." He laughs. "They keep it away from you. I think your fifth year they show you where the top secret material is."

I ask him which ice-cream dessert is the best, and he recommends the chocolate eclair. I buy one, and Matt and I continue on our way to the museum. The arched glass windows of the front entrance and the rockets outside give the whole area an aura of American might mixed with amusement park glee. Matt starts shooting footage with the Hi-8 camera.

We've had luck in the past finding people with UFO experiences just by showing up in the right places. We're hoping it will happen to us here. But who else besides the ice cream guy should we hassle? The museum shop seems like a good bet. It's filled with books, models, and the usual useless memorabilia. A painfully plain

Midwestern girl with mousy blonde hair stands behind the counter. She's wearing a brown checkered shirt. A sign that says, "PLEASE LET THE CASHIER KNOW HOW MANY POST CARDS YOU ARE PURCHASING" clings to the register.

I draw from my pocket a 3×5 card with a sticker of a Gray's head plastered on it.

"This fellow is a Gray alien," I explain to the check-out girl. "We were wondering if in all your time as an employee of Wright-Patterson Air Force Base you had ever encountered anything like this."

"No," she says, taken aback.

"Are you sure?" I ask.

"Yeah," she replies and nods for emphasis.

"You don't have any memory blanks or time lapses where you didn't know what you were doing, but you thought you were here? That sort of thing?" I inquire.

"No. Not yet, anyway. Not yet," she answers.

"And this job is exciting?" I query.

We make our first impression.

"Yeah."

"Involve a lot of training?"

"No, not really," she says. Her answers have become terse, and I notice tension building behind her brown eyes.

"They didn't take you underground into some secret area to show you what to do?"

"No."

"Obviously, we've got a serious case of denial, here, folks," I report to the camera.

"It's classified," she finally admits. "If I told you, I'd have to kill you."

She seems convinced we're up to no good, and unlike the huge number of interviewee hams we've encountered on our trip, the poor girl's conspicuously camera shy. We give up trying to find a decent interview subject and look at the gifts instead, discovering a bright yellow flying saucer displayed alongside the airplane models. According to the electric-blue box, the Electronic Soaring UFO has "Awesome Sounds and Lights." Is this part of Wright-Patterson history, we wonder, or just a decoy to throw us off the trail?

Decoy or not, the trail has clearly ended here. We leave the museum shop and drive around the base for a final look. Prominently posted on the chain-link fence is a large white sign with bright red letters. It reads, "WARNING. U.S. AIR FORCE INSTALLATION. IT IS UNLAWFUL TO ENTER THIS AREA WITHOUT THE PERMISSION OF THE INSTALLATION COMMISSIONER. WHILE ON THIS INSTALLATION ALL PERSONNEL AND PROPERTY UNDER THEIR CONTROL ARE SUBJECT TO SEARCH."

After Area 51, the sign seems less than intimidating. I can't help but wonder if, like the UFO model in the museum shop, the museum itself is a decoy to keep U.S. citizens out of the real Wright-Patterson.

It's been 34 days since we started this journey, and we're glad that it's over, at least for now. We leave Wright-Patterson behind us, and set off down the highway towards Pittsburgh, Pa., where we'll get some much-needed rest at the home of Matt's girlfriend, Cyndi.

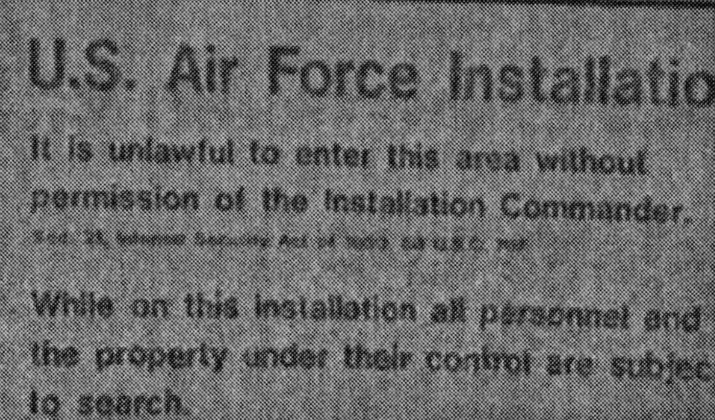

This means you.

Searching for Dr. Mack

Boston, Massachusetts
March 7, 1997
J.F.

It's early March, and I'm living in Somerville, Mass., scraping out a living teaching jazz part-time at Boston University and writing freelance music reviews for the *Boston Phoenix* and *Film Score Monthly.* Matt has retreated to New York, N.Y., where he's working as an editorial assistant for *Country Living* magazine. Our trip across America has been over for eight months, but our relationship with the UFO phenomenon is far from finished.

In Cambridge, Mass., a town located not ten minutes from my doorstep, the Gray Highway will end. While Boston's cross-river rival isn't a well known UFO hot spot, Dr. John Mack, professor, Pulitzer prize winner, noted psychiatrist, and author of *Abduction: Human Encounters with Aliens,* teaches at the city's world-famous institute of high-

NEW HAMPSHIRE
MASSACHUSETTS
BOSTON BAY
Boston

er learning, Harvard University. Matt and I have tried for close to a year to make first contact with John Mack, but the good doctor, so far, has remained elusive.

Our hunt for Dr. Mack began in late February of 1996. At the time, we had no idea what shape our cross-country trip would take, so we researched UFOs heavily: delving into books, searching the Internet, and watching television programs. I felt as if I had plunged my head into the murky depths of an algae-covered pond. The amount of confusing and contradictory information available on UFOs was truly frustrating.

Matt and I agreed we were not going to try to prove the UFO phenomenon true or false, real or unreal. Too many had attempted to do that before us and failed miserably. The purpose of our trip, we decided, was to gain a clearer picture of the people and the places involved. How does America appear through the lens of the UFO phenomenon? What type of people make up the population of UFO believers, watchers, and abductees? How do such people view life on this planet? How do their ideas differ from those of mainstream society? What are their lives like?

In his book *Abduction*, Dr. Mack presents case studies of 13 abductees, from a total of 76 he interviewed over a period of four years, beginning in 1990. Mack proposes a number of hypotheses based upon his research. The most important one, I believe, is that the traditional Western thought paradigm, which emphasizes "hard" science, is too confining to allow for the abduction experience. Alien abduction does not fall so easily into categories, and because Dr. Mack was not willing to discount the stories of his patients, his book caused a good deal of controversy.

Matt and I felt that Dr. Mack would be the ideal person to give us a sense of perspective on the UFO and alien abduction phenomenon before we went on our jaunt across America. Cambridge was not too far away from my college apartment in the student slums of Allston, Mass., but because Matt and I wanted to do this interview together, interaction with Dr. Mack would have to wait until Matt came to Boston. He planned to brave the cold North for spring break, providing us with the opportunity we needed.

Now, all we had to do was convince the doctor to talk with us. Our first query fax requesting an interview was either lost or ignored by Dr. Mack's office, but the second, sent from my Allston apartment on March 5, 1996, elicited a return call from one of Mack's assistants. The assistant admitted to some mild interest and asked Matt to fax over our writing clips, which we did. When our clips were greeted by days of silence, Matt called again only to be informed that Dr. Mack was too busy to be interviewed.

We were disappointed but not defeated. Matt planned to return to attend my Boston University graduation and help me move out of my apartment. We would have another chance to talk to the doctor. Matt faxed Mack's office from Penn State, mentioning the dates he would be in town. However, when May rolled around, Dr. Mack's office refused us again. This time they said the doctor was preoccupied with traveling and attending conferences. We would have to embark upon our journey without the benefit of his insight.

Nearly a year later, we are still on Dr. Mack's trail. Matt is pinned to a 9-to-5 job in New York City, so this time it's up to me to obtain an interview. My opportunity will come on Friday, March 7, 1997, when Dr. Mack is scheduled to appear with UFO abduction researcher and author, Budd Hopkins, to publicly discuss the topic of alien abduction at John Hancock Hall in Boston. The lecture, benefiting the Program for Extraordinary Experience Research (P.E.E.R.), which John Mack founded to investigate the alien abduction phenomenon, and the Intruder's Foundation, Budd Hopkins's similarly focused organization, will be hosted by National Public Radio journalist Christopher Lydon.

The first step for me, then, is to buy a ticket for the event, which proves to be more difficult than it sounds. When I call P.E.E.R., I am told by an operator that employees of the organization are not allowed to give out the address over the phone. Instead, I need to give them my address, and they will send all the information I need regarding the lecture. This seems a little surreal to me, but I oblige the operator with my address, understanding that certain precautions must be taken in order to protect the privacy of alien abductees who visit P.E.E.R. Nevertheless, when I receive a notice in the mail a few days later, I can't help but wonder if P.E.E.R. isn't a little bit inconsistent. The organization's address is printed for all to see on the front of the envelope. I hastily tear open the letter and discover, to my dismay, two uninformative pieces of paper. One has a list of good restaurants to visit and hotels to stay at, if you're from out of town. The other gives directions on how to get to John Hancock Hall. Granted, this would be wonderful information, if I needed any of it, but all I want to do is buy a ticket. Neither of the sheets provides me with the admission price or the time the lecture starts. I call back P.E.E.R. and this time the answering machine picks up. An automated message informs me that the program begins at 7:30 P.M. I also learn that tickets cost $20 in advance and $30 at the door, which is a little steep on a freelance writer's budget of nothing. It's Thursday, and there's no way I can order a ticket in advance anymore. But this quest to meet Dr. Mack has almost reached religious proportions. A sense of closure might be worth the cash.

Fortunately, Fate or something similar lends a hand. On Friday, I run into two of my more memorable college professors, who are producing a play about alien abduction. They share my interest in UFOs, will be attending the lecture, and have a working relationship of sorts with P.E.E.R. Apparently, P.E.E.R. wants some shots of the pre-lecture meet-and-greet with Mack and Hopkins. If I can find someone to take pictures backstage, the photographer and I can get into the lecture for free. At last, the opportunity to meet Dr. Mack has come. It's nearly 5:00 P.M., so I make a frantic phone call to Hunter Boyle, a friend of mine with photography experience and a good camera. Hunter is mildly curious about alien abduction and agrees to meet me at the T (trolley) stop on Commonwealth

Avenue. I rush to CVS, buy a couple rolls of film, and hustle to the T stop. Hunter's car soon arrives, and I jump aboard. We're on our way.

John Hancock Hall's lobby is swarming with people, all who, unlike us, seem to know where they're going. At this point, I'm skeptical about whether or not Hunter and I will be able to get into the lecture, and it seems I have every right to be. The attendants at the press table have no idea who we are. I explain our situation as best I can, and they are kind enough to give us press kits and badges. However, we will not be able to go backstage by our-selves. Apparently, we'll have to wait until someone can escort us. Hunter and I take this opportunity to duck into a stairwell so he can load film into his camera without get-ting jostled. When we return to the lobby a few moments later, I see one of my college professors emerging from the mass of people. He indicates that we should follow him, and Hunter and I squeeze our way through the crowd, past the doors, and into the lecture hall.

Compared to the chaos outside in the lobby, the hall is pleasantly quiet. The room slopes downward towards a wide stage. In the aisles, a few technicians fiddle with the video camera tripods, three-legged media Cyclopes star-ing blankly forward. As we amble towards the stage, I notice that a large section of the seats in front have been roped off for the press. We climb the steps and then slip behind the closed curtains.

Emerging on the other side, Hunter and I find ourselves hip-deep in pre-lecture reception. I feel immensely out of place; a young, untried writer in worn jeans and T-shirt

BACKSTAGE
WITH THE
DOCTOR

970307

trying to mingle with the academic-looking, formally clad guests. This atmosphere is a far cry from the halls of Unarius or the beaches of Pensacola. I scan the room and spot Dr. Mack chatting with admirers by the refreshment table. After a year of tracking the elusive doctor, I've finally found him. But, what to do now? For a moment, I debate blasting into his conversation, delivering one poignant question after another, then quickly discard the notion. My normally supple interviewer's mind has frozen itself solid. I can't remember anything I want to ask the doctor. The hell with it. I'll just improvise.

Unfortunately, I'm ill prepared when the moment comes. My college professor does his part, catching the doctor's attention and introducing Hunter and myself. I figure I have three seconds to blurt out "Good to meet you, Dr. Mack. I took a trip across the country to famous UFO sites last summer and would like to discuss it with you." Not a chance. Before one word can pass my lips, the doctor gracefully nods "hello," turns, and is gone, already on his way to speak with some other party.

I've missed my first opportunity, but I am still determined to get one quote from Dr. Mack. I seize a bottle of apple juice from the refreshment table to pump up my blood sugar and bolster my courage for another pass. Hunter's camera clicks away as he photographs what is proving, for me at least, to be a very frustrating gathering. Then, without warning, the soiree is over, and event staff hustle us offstage. I can't believe it. I was so close. I reluctantly take a seat by my professors. Hunter has situated himself in the media pit so he can snap a few more pictures. By my count, there are more than 500 people in the hall, with a median age of about 40 years old.

Onstage, the setting is stark and formal. To the right side, three chairs, three end tables, two lamps, and a coffee table are all carefully arranged on top of an elegant rug, "fireside chat" style. On the left side is the lecture podium.

The audience applauds loudly as Christopher Lydon, a white-haired and white-bearded gentleman, steps up to the podium. The fact that Lydon, a well-recognized and respected figure in the Boston area, has agreed to host this event is testimony to the degree to which curiosity about UFOs and alien abduction has grown. Much like John Mack, and to a lesser extent Budd Hopkins, Lydon risks losing professional credibility by taking the investigation of alien abductions seriously.

In his opening remarks, Lydon introduces the key speakers and establishes his role as the mediator, the skeptic. The focus of the evening, Lydon explains, will be upon defining the reality of UFO abductions. Are these abductions occurring in our physical reality or are they similar, in many ways, to our dreams?

Budd Hopkins will be the first investigator to speak. An artist and author of the books *Missing Time, Intruders,* and *Witnessed: The True Story of the Brooklyn Bridge UFO Abductions,* Hopkins introduced John Mack to the alien abduction phenomenon in 1990.

Hopkins's voice is less forceful than Lydon's, and it's difficult to hear him through the sound system. However, before Hopkins can even finish his first thought, cries of

Dr. John Mack (left) joins Budd Hopkins (center) and Christopher Lydon (right).

"Turn it up!", "We can't hear you back here!", and "Much louder please!" surge through the room. Hopkins leans towards the microphone, and feedback sings through the speakers. Whines, moans, and complaints erupt from the audience, not unlike the response of moviegoers when a picture wobbles on the screen. The academic formality of the proceedings seems lost, and I wonder whether the serious investigation of the UFO phenomenon has come very far, after all. In less than 30 seconds, the audience has turned this meeting into a circus sideshow.

To Hopkins' credit, he is unshaken by the boisterous response. He continues with his speech, beginning by saying he respects John Mack for his courage and appreciates the difficulty Mack underwent by bringing such an unconventional subject to the attention of "a university," presumably Harvard. "I think any human being in this room would have to admit that, if the UFO phenomenon is occurring as the reports suggest, it's the most important event in human history," Hopkins states. "And if that's the case, I don't think any institution or organization would be very wise to oppose the serious investigation of such a phenomenon."

It's clear the two alien abduction investigators appreciate each other's work. When it's John Mack's turn to speak, he attempts to defuse the notion that there is a polarity of viewpoints between himself and Hopkins. Mack believes the abductions may take place in a separate reality, while Hopkins believes in the physical nature of the phenomenon. Mack explains, in his lecture, that alien abduction defies categorization. "It doesn't lend its secrets to the methods that we know," Mack states. He also says that, for the abductees, the phenomenon seems as impossible and improbable as it does to everyone else, which raises an important question: Why is there so much resistance to discovering the truth behind the abductions?

After Mack and Hopkins finish, they open the floor for questions. Audience members line up, at least five deep, behind two microphones, positioned four-fifths of the way down the auditorium's side aisles. However, true to P.E.E.R.'s policy, even in this open forum, there is an element of secrecy present, ostensibly to protect the identities of the questioners: One line of people will be recorded by the video camera, the other will not.

The audience is an interesting cross-section of the UFO community, a mix of concerned, scholarly types and patently strange individuals. The man sitting in front of me falls into the latter category. He's wearing a pastel-colored silk shirt and a diamond on a chain around his neck. Attached to the chain is a jeweler's glass, apparently present so that admirers, like the woman sitting next to him, can examine the precious stone.

An evening with P.E.E.R.

The Q&A session quickly turns ugly, talk-show style, with all the prerequisite grandstanding and nonsensical babbling. Most of the audience members preface their questions with drawn-out preambles, and I can feel a deep-seated sense of frustration grow among those who would rather hear Mack, Hopkins, and Lydon say a word or two. As a whole, the evening is shot. Dr. Mack has become agitated and begins ducking questions, stating that audience members are addressing alien abduction on too literal a level. "We have to be more sophisticated about our definition of reality," he says. Hunter and I are glad when the night is over.

Three days later, Hunter's photographs come back from the developer. Most of them are blurry, not unlike all the UFO pictures I've ever seen. However, there are one or two usable ones. I give P.E.E.R. a call, and the publicist says they're interested in the photos. I leave my name and number, but they never get back to me. Since P.E.E.R is affiliated with the Department of Psychiatry at the Cambridge Hospital, where Matt and I sent our original interview requests for Dr. Mack, somehow I'm not surprised.

So, without even a courtesy call at the desk, our American UFO tour ends. But Matt and I have not completed our adventure unchanged.

John Mack explains in *Abduction: Human Encounters with Aliens* that "Because of the relative thinness of the physical findings, however genuine, a heavy burden of evidence for the reality of the abduction phenomenon falls upon the reported experiences, or 'witnessing' of the experiencers themselves."

Although certainly not researchers of Mack's stature or "experiencers," like Mack's patients, Matt and I, in many ways, are witnesses to the variety of people affected by the UFO phenomenon. We've stood on the beach and stared at the sky over Gulf Breeze, Fla., on a clear night. We've seen the tourist game in Roswell, N.Mex. and stood among the spiritual/magnetic vortices of Sedona, Ariz. We've peered at the mysterious hangars of Area 51, and talked with an abductee whose interaction with aliens has utterly changed her life. While none of our firsthand experiences have come close to tapping the source, and neither of us can lay claim to even having seen one mysterious light, somehow I still feel like we've seen the evidence. As Dr. Mack suggests in *Abduction,* the Western thought paradigm doesn't even begin to allow for the UFO experience. UFOs stretch our imaginations to their limits.

There are many who believe UFOs are real. We've spoken to them, we've heard them speak, and they've shown

HARVARD MEDICAL SCHOOL

JOHN E. MACK, M.D.
PROFESSOR OF PSYCHIATRY

THE CAMBRIDGE HOSPITAL

█████████ STREET
CAMBRIDGE, MASSACHUSETTS 02139

June 23, 1998

Mr. Jonathan L. Follett
████████████████████████
Brighton, Ma   02135

Dear Mr. Follett:

    Thank you very much for your invitation to write a preface for your work on the UFO phenomenon in America. My own writing committments at the present time make it impossible to take on another. Again, I appreciate your thinking of me and wish you the best with your book.

Sincerely,

John E. Mack, M.D.

The chase ends.

us a glimpse of what's out there. Because of them, we've been able to see the heart of a mystery and, for us, for now, that's enough.

238

About the Authors

Jonathan Follett lives, works, and plays music in Boston.
Matthew Holm lives, works, and draws in New York City.
They are currently preparing a book about the apocalypse.
They hope to finish it before the world ends.

Matt

Jon

Order Gray Highway

Visit www.strangevoices.com or order by mail.

You may clip and use this order form or photocopy it.

Please send me _____ copies of *Gray Highway: An American UFO Journey*.

Subtotal _______________ ($11.95 × # of books)

Sales Tax _____________ (NY residents add $0.99 per book for sales tax)

Total _____________

Mr./Ms. ____

Address ____

City _______________________ State __________ Zip ________

E-mail ____

Send check or money order. No cash or C.O.D.'s.

Make checks payable to:

    Toadspittle Hill Productions

    Radio City Station

    P.O. Box 1846

    New York, NY 10101-1846

Please allow four to six weeks for delivery. Price and availability subject to change without notice.